Contents

2nd edition

IELTS

to success

preparation tips and practice tests

HAWTHORN
ENGLISH LANGUAGE CENTRES

Janina Tucker and Eric van Bemmel

John Wiley & Sons Australia, Ltd

First published 1997 by
John Wiley & Sons Australia, Ltd
33 Park Road, Milton, Qld 4064

Offices also in Sydney and Melbourne

Typeset in 11/13 pt Cg Caslon

Second edition 2002

© John Wiley & Sons Australia, Ltd 2002

IELTS to success: preparation tips & practice tests.

2nd ed.
ISBN 0 470 80180 8.

1. International English Language Testing System.
2. English language — Examinations, questions, etc.
3. English language — Textbooks for foreign speakers.
4. English language — Australia — Study and teaching — Foreign
speakers. 5. English language — Problems, exercises, etc.
I. Hawthorn English Language Centres. II. Title:
International English Language Testing System to success.

428.0076

The authors take no responsibility for the factual
accuracy or the views expressed in the listening
scripts and reading passages in this book.

Art by Paul Lennon

Cover and internal images © 2001 Artville

Printed in Singapore by
Kyodo Printing Co (S'pore) Pte Ltd

10 9 8 7 6 5 4 3 2

What's inside IELTS to Success

IELTS to Success is designed to help you prepare for the IELTS (International English Language Testing System) examination by providing strategies and material for practice in all areas of the test. *IELTS to Success* is aimed specifically at people taking the IELTS Academic Module rather than the General Training Module (for more information, see the Introduction, page 1).

The Introduction provides an overview of IELTS for readers not familiar with the test. It contains a breakdown of each section of the examination, including content and procedure.

The Skills and Strategies section discusses skills that are especially important in sitting IELTS. We suggest you look through this section to help you identify any skill areas in which you may need to improve. This section will also help you become familiar with the kinds of instructions and tasks found in IELTS tests. The listening tasks in this section can be heard on Audio Cassette One, Side A, of the audio cassettes that have been developed to accompany this book. (These cassettes are available as separate sale items or they can be obtained by purchasing the book and cassette package, which is also available.)

Of particular importance in the Skills and Strategies section are the pages focusing on the Speaking Module. The Speaking test is done as a one-to-one live interview, now in revised format to ensure that the interview conditions are the same for all candidates. We take a comprehensive look at what is expected of you in the interview and offer various language strategies and tips we have found to be useful. We recommend that you set up a practice interview with a teacher or a friend who speaks good English and get some feedback on your performance.

The next sections are made up of practice papers for the IELTS Listening, Reading and Writing Modules. There are three complete Practice Listening papers, to be done while listening to the audio cassettes that accompany this book. They are followed by six Practice Reading papers and six Practice Writing papers.

Finally, we provide answers for the Practice Listening and Reading papers and sample answers for the Practice Writing papers, followed by tapescripts for the Listening papers.

IELTS to Success contains many ideas and useful practice material that will help you to improve your performance on the IELTS test. If you have an opportunity, we recommend you also take an IELTS Preparation class at a Hawthorn English Language Centre. The practice gained in working in a structured program with other students will provide additional motivation and support and help you progress more quickly.

Preface

Vancouver, Canada

Melbourne, Australia

Edinburgh, Scotland

Hawthorn English Language Centre — Melbourne

IELTS to Success has been developed by staff at the Hawthorn English Language Centre — Melbourne.

Hawthorn–Melbourne is the English Language Centre of the University of Melbourne. The Centre, which has been operating since 1986, specialises in preparing international students for university study in Australia. Hawthorn–Melbourne has developed a number of English for Academic Purposes and examination preparation programs over the years with the goal of providing international students with the English language and study skills required for successful tertiary study.

Hawthorn–Melbourne is also an award-winning IELTS testing facility, having received the IELTS Australia 1998 Major City Award for its contribution to the continued success of IELTS in Australia and internationally. The IELTS exam is held regularly on the campus.

The Hawthorn Network

Hawthorn–Melbourne is part of an international network of high-quality English schools initiated by the University of Melbourne. Members of the Hawthorn English Language Centres Network are high-quality English schools, each with a deserved reputation for excellence in teaching, curriculum and student services. The schools operate independently, retaining their individual characteristics, but are united by a commitment to putting the needs and goals of students first.

For further information on the network, visit the web site at:
www.hawthornenglish.com

Auckland, New Zealand

Acknowledgements

IELTS to Success was developed and trialled at the Hawthorn English Language Centre — Melbourne. Janina Tucker wrote the Skills and Strategies section and provided updated material on Speaking skills for this revised edition. Eric van Bemmel wrote the practice Listening, Reading and Writing papers, with assistance from Greg Deakin, who worked on the project as a consulting editor.

The authors are indebted to Kathleen Lynch for her substantial contributions to *IELTS to Success*. Thanks also to Don Oliver for his assistance with illustration briefs and for advice on skills and strategies for the revised Speaking Module in the current edition.

The authors would also like to express their gratitude to the following people for support and encouragement during the planning and writing of this book: Robert Travers, Jackie Woodroffe, Elaine Billington, John Cunningham, Katie Keane, Ben Stubbs and Kerri Atkinson.

The trialling of the practice test papers and the production of the trial versions of the accompanying tapes were completed with the generous contribution of time by our colleagues: Pat Connor, Andrea Flew, Charles Kerstjens, Patrick McLaughlin, Pat McRitchie, Cynthia Ong, Barbara Semmler, Paul Shea, Trish Stewart, John Sutton, Rob Youngs and Lynn McVeigh.

The authors especially wish to acknowledge Suzette, Reuben, Chris, Kathryn, Stephen and Sarah for their patience and understanding over the many hours it took to produce this book.

The authors and publisher are grateful to the following individuals and organisations for permission to reproduce copyright material: A. B. and J. W. Cribb, *Wild Food in Australia*, William Collins, Sydney, 1975, adapted with the permission of Harper-Collins Publishers; Michael Replogle (contact at www.environmentaldefense.org), 'Non-Motorized Vehicles in Asia: Strategies for Management', presented at the Supercities of the Pacific Rim Conference, October 1992, Centre for Renewable Energy & Sustainable Technology.

For the photographs of the Hawthorn English Language Centres that accompany the Preface (p. *vi*), the following sources are acknowledged:
Auckland: MEI New Zealand and photographer Michael Stephen; Vancouver: Hawthorn English Language Centre — Canada; Edinburgh: Steve Godfrey, Redwing Pictures; Melbourne: Louise Reynolds.

Introduction

to the IELTS test

IELTS, the International English Language Testing System, is a test for students who must demonstrate English language proficiency to gain entry to universities or training programs in English-speaking countries. For overseas candidates wishing to study in tertiary institutions in the United Kingdom or Australia, in particular, IELTS is the most widely recognised assessment of English language proficiency.

Candidates planning university study should take the IELTS Academic Module. Candidates wishing to enrol in vocational training or secondary school should take the IELTS General Training Module. The two modules differ only in the reading and writing subtests; listening and speaking subtests are the same. *Please note that this text does not provide practice specifically for the General Training Module.*

Candidates do not pass or fail IELTS. Within two weeks of sitting the IELTS test, candidates receive their results in the form of 'band scores' (see page 6 for more information on band scores). The band scores are also sent to the learning institution to which the candidate has applied. The relevant department or faculty determines if the candidate's band score is of an acceptable level for admission to study.

The IELTS test is divided into four parts, called 'modules' or 'subtests'. The modules, in the sequence a candidate sits them, are shown below. The entire test takes around 2 hours and 45 minutes.

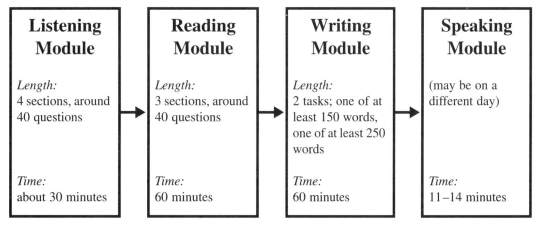

Listening Module	**Reading Module**	**Writing Module**	**Speaking Module**
Length: 4 sections, around 40 questions	*Length:* 3 sections, around 40 questions	*Length:* 2 tasks; one of at least 150 words, one of at least 250 words	(may be on a different day)
Time: about 30 minutes	*Time:* 60 minutes	*Time:* 60 minutes	*Time:* 11–14 minutes

The IELTS Listening Module

This module consists of four taped sections of increasing difficulty. The Listening Module typically has two dialogues and two monologues. The tape is played once only.

Sections 1 and 2 normally involve speakers talking about social situations and needs. For example, there may be a conversation between a university student and a landlord, or a monologue about a city's public transport system.

Sections 3 and 4 reflect a more 'educational' context. For example, you may hear a group of students discussing their lecture notes. Or you may hear part of a lecturer's talk on a given subject. (Remember that the Listening Module is not assessing your knowledge of any particular subject. There is no need to feel anxious if the topic of the conversation or monologue is not familiar.)

Your task is to answer questions as you listen to the tape. For each section, you will hear a (taped) announcer introducing the situation. You are then given a short period (up to 30 seconds) to read through the questions for that section. As the conversation or monologue proceeds, work through the questions. When the section finishes, you will be given an additional 30 seconds to check your work. Each section follows this pattern.

In the actual IELTS test, you are permitted to write your answers on the question paper. At the end of Section 4 of the Listening Module, you will be asked to transfer your answers from the question paper to an answer sheet. You will be given about ten minutes to transfer your answers. (Note that no answer sheets for the Practice Listening Subtests are contained in this book.)

There are several types of questions you can expect in the Listening Module. These include:

- short answer
- multiple choice
- matching
- referring to a map
- completing sentences

- completing notes
- completing a summary
- completing a table
- completing a form
- completing a flow chart or diagram.

Sample answers are sometimes provided in the IELTS Listening Module.

Although you should expect the types of questions listed above, this does not mean you will have to answer each type. The IELTS Listening Module contains a combination of some or all of the listed types, but the combination changes from test to test. In other words, you can never be sure exactly which question types you will have to answer on any given test date.

The types of skills the Listening Module assesses include:

- identifying the gist of a conversation or monologue
- extracting specific factual information
- identifying speaker roles
- identifying relationships between ideas or pieces of information, such as:
  – cause and effect
  – order of events
  – comparison
- following directions and instructions
- identifying numbers, dates, time etc.
- making inferences
- determining when a speaker is expressing fact, assumption or opinion.

The Listening Module must be taken together with the Reading and Writing Modules.

> • *You will find tips and practice sections for the Listening Module on pages 7–16.*
>
> • *Practice subtests for the Listening Module begin on page 43.*

 # The IELTS Reading Module

This module consists of three reading passages of increasing difficulty, each accompanied by questions. Each reading passage is between 500 and 900 words. You are given 60 minutes to answer questions for all three passages.

The reading passages are on a variety of subjects and are chosen for their suitability for candidates entering university. For example, a passage may discuss alternative energy projects or perhaps report on research into management trends. The passages may contain information presented in the form of tables, diagrams, charts and so on. A short glossary of technical words may accompany reading passages.

Questions generally follow the reading passages to which they refer, but occasionally questions occur before a reading passage. (Remember that the Reading Module is not assessing your knowledge of any particular subject. There is no need to feel anxious if the topic of the passage is not familiar.)

Your task is to answer the questions based on the reading passages. You must place your answers directly on the answer sheet, although you are free to make marks, such as underlining, on the question paper. (Note that a photocopyable answer sheet for the practice reading papers can be found on page 65.)

There are several types of questions you can expect in the Reading Module. These include:

- short answer
- multiple choice
- matching
- classification
- completing sentences
- completing notes
- completing a summary
- completing a table
- completing a form
- completing a flow chart or diagram
- selecting headings for paragraphs and sections
- recognising a writer's views or claims.

Sample answers are sometimes provided in the IELTS Reading Module.

Although you should expect the types of questions listed above, that does not mean you will have to answer each type. The IELTS Reading Module contains a combination of some of the listed types, but the combination changes from test to test. You can never be sure which question types you will have to answer on any given test date.

The types of skills the Reading Module assesses include:
- identifying the gist of a passage
- finding detailed factual information in a passage
- identifying relationships between ideas or information items, such as:
  – cause and effect
  – order of events
  – comparison
- making inferences
- distinguishing between fact, assumption or opinion
- understanding text organisation
- summarising information.

The Reading Module must be taken together with the Listening and Writing Modules.

- *You will find tips and practice sections for the Reading Module on pages 16–24.*
- *Practice subtests for the Reading Module begin on page 64.*

 # The IELTS Writing Module

This module consists of two activities, Writing Task 1 and Writing Task 2. You are given 60 minutes to complete both tasks.

In **Writing Task 1**, you are asked to describe information that is usually presented in the form of a graph, table or diagram. You may be asked to do one of the following:
- organise and present the information
- make a comparison between two or more sets of data
- describe how something works
- explain a process or procedure.

You must write a minimum of 150 words for Task 1. It is recommended that you spend about 20 minutes.

In **Writing Task 2**, you are asked to:
- put forward a point of view on a given topic
- argue in support of or against a given statement
- propose a solution to a given problem
- speculate on implications of a given issue.

You must write a minimum of 250 words for Task 2. It is recommended that you spend about 40 minutes.

The writing tasks are on a variety of subjects and are chosen for their suitability for candidates entering university. For example, you may be asked to describe a graph comparing working hours in different countries (Task 1), or you may be asked if you agree that technology is destructive to traditional societies and to give your reasons (Task 2).

In the actual IELTS test, you must write your answers in essay or report form on the Writing Module answer sheet. You are permitted to make marks, such as a plan or outline, on the question paper. (Note that no answer sheets for the practice writing subtests are contained in this book.)

The Writing Module must be taken together with the Listening and Reading Modules.

> • *You will find tips and strategies for the Writing Module on pages 25–34.*
>
> • *Practice subtests for the Writing Module begin on page 129.*

 # The IELTS Speaking Module

This module consists of a one-to-one interview with an examiner.

The interview lasts between 11 and 14 minutes and is divided into three parts:

Part 1. Introduction and interview

Here you will be introduced to the examiner and your name and identity will be checked. As a warm-up to the remainder of this part, you will be asked a series of questions that relate to your own personal life. These will be closely followed by further questions, also based on familiar topics, that cover a slightly wider range of experiences.

In Part 1, the examiner can repeat the question only once, as he or she must adhere to a predetermined script. The examiner is not allowed to explain the question to you.

This part normally takes four to five minutes.

Part 2. Individual long turn

In this part, the examiner will give you a topic and ask you to talk about it for one to two minutes. You will be told that you have one minute to prepare your ideas and you will be given some paper and a pencil for making notes about the given topic. You will also be presented with a Candidate Task Sheet, which tells you what to describe and what details you should include in your short presentation.

After one minute, the examiner will ask you to begin. At the end of your presentation, the examiner may ask you one or two questions related to your talk in order to complete this part of the test.

Including preparation time, this part usually takes three to four minutes.

Part 3. Two-way discussion

Here, the examiner will encourage you to discuss a series of more general questions related by theme to the topic you spoke about in Part 2. The discussion typically goes into some depth in this part; the examiner will often ask questions that are quite abstract and that require complex answers.

This part of the test normally takes four to five minutes.

The examiner will then thank you, and that will signal the end of your speaking test.

• Remember that the Speaking Module is not assessing your knowledge of any particular subject. There is no need to feel anxious that a speaking topic might be unfamiliar to you.

• Your interview will be recorded on audio cassette.

> • *You will find a more detailed description of the Speaking Module, together with tips and strategies, on pages 35–41.*

IELTS test results

You will receive your results within two weeks. Results are given in the form of band scores. One band score is given for each of the four IELTS modules. An overall band score is calculated from these four band scores.

Band scores range from 1 to 9. A band score 1 means the candidate has essentially no ability to use English. A band score 9 indicates the candidate is a fluent and accurate user of English, much like an educated native speaker. A band score of 0 is given only when a candidate does not attempt the test. For entrance to university in countries such as Australia and the United Kingdom, overall band scores of between 6 and 7 are usually acceptable. Some university faculties require that band scores for each of the four IELTS modules meet a given minimum level.

An IELTS test result may look something like this:

Test results				
Listening	Band	6.5		
Reading	Band	6.5		
Writing	Band	7.0		
Speaking	Band	6.0	OVERALL BAND	6.5

Frequently asked questions about IELTS

- *What IELTS band score do I need to get into university?*
  You must find out what score you need from the relevant faculty or department of the university to which you are applying. Do not ask IELTS test examiners or officials as they will not be able to give you a precise answer.
- *Can the IELTS test be taken more than once?*
  Yes, but you must wait three months before sitting the test again.
- *Do I have to do all four IELTS modules on the same day?*
  No. The Speaking Module can sometimes be done on a separate day. Check with your nearest IELTS test centre. The Listening, Reading and Writing Modules must be done together.
- *Is it necessary to do all four IELTS modules?*
  Yes. University faculties are often interested in how you do in each of the four modules. Also, the overall band score cannot be calculated unless all four subtests have been completed.
- *Which IELTS module should I do, the Academic or the General Training Module?*
  It depends on your study plans. If you intend to enter university either as an undergraduate or as a postgraduate student, then you must take the Academic Module. On the other hand, if you are planning to enter a vocational training program or secondary school, the General Training Module is usually sufficient. If in doubt, contact the learning institution to which you are applying.
- *How long will it take to get my results?*
  Normally, you will receive your results within 2 weeks.

Skills and Strategies
for IELTS

The following section of the book tells you about the skills and strategies required to do well in the IELTS test. There are various exercises that help you to review the skills and offer useful strategies. The correct answers and explanations are also given.

 ## Skills for the Listening Module

In the IELTS Listening Module, the recording is played once only. You must, therefore, use a number of strategies to help you listen closely. You will need four main skills to do well in the IELTS Listening Module. These are:

1. **Understanding the instructions**
Instructions are **both written** on the question paper and spoken on the tape. Read and listen to every word in the instructions very carefully. Ensure that you follow them exactly and answer in the correct way.

2. **Previewing and predicting**
An announcer will briefly outline:

- the topic
- who is talking
- the situation.

Try to listen carefully as this will help you to preview the questions.

Before the recording begins for each section, you will be given up to 30 seconds to read and become familiar with the questions. Use this time efficiently so that you can prepare yourself to listen for the information you need.

Here are some hints for previewing and predicting:

- Study the question carefully and try to predict what type of answer is required. For example, will it be a date, a name or maybe a number?
- Check the differences between similar-looking pictures or diagrams.
- Look for minor details such as different numbers or omissions.

In addition to the 30 seconds before each section, you will also be given 30 seconds after each section to look over your answers. If you are satisfied with your answers in the section you have just finished, move on to the next section and use the full 60 seconds for previewing.

3. Listening for specific information

Use of previewing and predicting skills will help you listen for the specific information you need to answer the questions in the Listening Module. Listening for key words and common connective words often helps to signal the specific information that you need in order to answer the question. (See the lists of words provided on page 18.) Make sure that while you are actually writing your answers, you continue to listen to the information given in the recordings as there will not be a second opportunity to hear it.

4. Checking and rewriting

You are given about 30 seconds after each section to check your answers. Check that all your answers correspond with the given instructions.

Make sure that you have answered *every* question. Marks are not deducted for incorrect answers so, if you are unsure of a particular answer, you should guess by writing down what you think is the most likely answer.

Check that you have included only what is necessary in the answer.

At the end of the Listening Module, you are given about 10 minutes to transfer your answers from the question paper onto the answer sheet. Scan your answers to ensure that you have transferred them correctly, so that the number on the question paper corresponds with the number on the answer sheet. Be especially careful when transferring answers from tables as sometimes the items are not ordered linearly.

 # Practice for the Listening Module

The following two exercises are designed to help you practise some of the skills required in the Listening Module. Carry out the exercises then read the answers and explanations that follow them.

Before you listen to the recording for the 'Listening Skills Practice' (on Audio Cassette One, Side A), look over Questions 1–7 for Listening Skills Practice 1 (pages 9–11). Check the following points when previewing the questions:

- I have read the instructions carefully.
- I know what form the answer must take.
- I have a good idea of what the recording is about.
- I have predicted some of the vocabulary I might hear by putting pictures or diagrams into words. For example, in question 1 on page 10, I said to myself the words 'car', 'double-decker bus', 'train', 'bus'.
- I have predicted the type of information I am looking for. For example, in Questions 4–7 on page 11:

> Question 4 = number of people
> Question 5 = an adjective describing injuries
> Question 6 = name of a transport line
> Question 7 = number of hours.

- I have anticipated some of the answers in the gap-filling questions by looking at the words before and after the gaps. I have used other clues, such as context or grammar, to help me predict the information for which I am listening.
- I know what information I need to listen for.

Questions 1–7

In Question 1, decide which picture best fits what you hear on the tape and circle the letter under that picture.

> *Example:* Which type of transport has caused the traffic problems?

A

B

Ⓒ

D

1.   How will passengers waiting to travel be transported now?

A

B

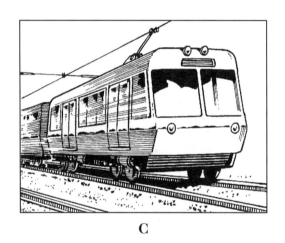

C

D

2.   What signs should drivers in the area look for?

Circle the correct answer.

DERAILMENT	SPECIAL BUSES
A	B

DETOUR	INTERSECTION
C	D

3.   Where did the accident occur?

Circle the letter indicating the correct location.

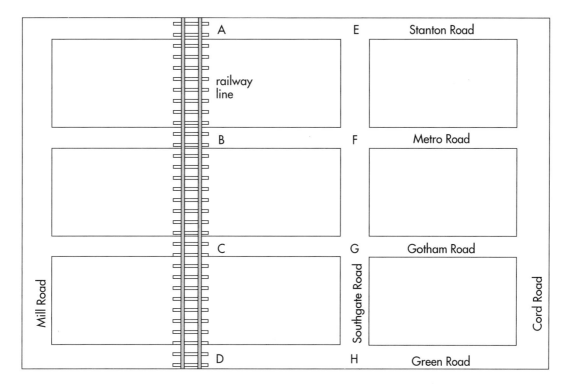

*Fill in the gaps for Questions 4–7 with **NO MORE THAN ONE WORD** and/or **NUMBER** for each gap.*

4.   Approximately .... people have been admitted to Riversdale Hospital.

5.   Dr Cross believes the people taken to hospital are suffering .... injuries.

6.   Metropolitan Transport is not yet able to reopen the .... Line.

7.   It will be closed for no more than ....

Questions 8–13

Complete the table with information from the conversation you hear on the tape. Write a **NUMBER** *or* **NO MORE THAN THREE WORDS** *for each answer.*

	VACANCY 1	*VACANCY 2*	*VACANCY 3*
TYPE OF JOB	*Example* *… Sales …* *… Representative …*	Receptionist	**(12)** … … …
SALARY	$140 per week	**(10)** … … …	$350+ per week
HOURS (MON–FRI)	**(8)** … … …	not given	5 a.m.–1 p.m.
QUALIFICATION OR TRAINING	none required	**(11)** … … …	apprenticeship completed
TELEPHONE NUMBER	**(9)** … … …	3663 4674	3842 7473
CODE	Q3497	not given	**(13)** … … …

Answers and explanations

Example. **C.** 'Train' is the correct answer because 'there has been a minor train derailment'.

1. **B.** Double-decker buses are buses with two levels. 'Special double-decker buses are now taking passengers who were hoping to travel on that line ...'

2. **C.** Detour sign. '... police ... have also asked motorists ... to be aware of the detour signs ...'

3. **C.** '... the accident site, which is on the Greenhill Line where the railway line actually crosses Gotham Road.'

4. **13.** The answer '20' would not be correct as that is how many people were treated at the scene. A further *thirteen* were taken to the Riversdale Hospital.

5. **Minor.** 'Serious' is not correct because they were 'lucky to have escaped serious harm and appear ... to be suffering only *minor* injuries.'

6. **Greenhill.** '... the Greenhill Line is not open at present ...'

7. **6 hours.** '... the line will be closed *for up to* 6 hours ...' 'for up to' has the same meaning as 'no more than' in this context.

When previewing Questions 8–13 did you:

- note that no answer may contain more than three words?
- check the different categories that will be discussed?
- try to predict the most likely order that the recording would take?

---

8. **6 p.m.–8 p.m.** '... from six till eight in the evening'.

9. **3556 7792.** The numbers must be in this order.

10. **$400 per week.** 'We're looking at ... about $400 a week.'

11. **(Some) computer skills/able to type/word processing (course).** These are three alternative answers. Any one of these could be given, but no more than *three words* must be used.

12. **Baker.** Although both 'baker' and 'bakery' are mentioned, the word for the *type of job* is required.

13. **R1648.** The program presenter alerts us to the forthcoming answer by saying, 'Well, I'm afraid we still need the *code* and phone number.' Be aware of key words that are mentioned, such as 'code', as these alert you to the information for which you need to listen.

If you need more help with the answers for Questions 1–13, read the tapescripts of the recording for Listening Skills Practice 1 and 2, which are provided on pages 14–16.

Listening skills PRACTICE 1 — TAPESCRIPT

ANNOUNCER: In a moment, you are going to hear a traffic report given by Elaine Wilson. Before you listen, look at Questions 1–7. Note the example that has been done for you.

PROGRAM PRESENTER: And now a word on the traffic. Elaine Wilson presents the latest traffic report.

ELAINE: Thank you, Michael. Traffic appears to be flowing steadily in most areas. Traffic on the Kingston and F63 freeways is moving well. The Astron and Victoria freeways are also reporting a good flow. There is one major area, however, which is causing great problems for peak hour traffic in the Gotham area, just north of Riversdale. There has been a minor train derailment on the Greenhill Line. Reports indicate that the last carriage of the train appears to have gone off the tracks. The extent of the damage is not known at this stage, nor is the number of casualties. Special double-decker buses are now taking passengers who were hoping to travel on that line, and traffic is being diverted around the problem area. The roads are very congested so police are warning motorists to avoid the Gotham area if at all possible. They have also asked motorists who must travel in the area to be aware of the detour signs which have been erected. There is an alternative route which avoids the accident area and which Metropolitan Transport officials believe will help to ease the problem with traffic in the area.

The main area of concern is around the accident site, which is on the Greenhill Line where the railway line actually crosses Gotham Road. The derailed train carriage is still blocking Gotham Road and the boom gates are down. Other roads, including Stanton and Metro Roads, have also been closed off to traffic in the locality.

ANNOUNCER: Now look at Questions 4–7. (*Pause*)

ELAINE WILSON: Now, there's just been an update on the Greenhill train derailment. It is believed that up to twenty people have been treated on the scene by an emergency medical team. A further thirteen people have been taken to the Riversdale Hospital for observation. Dr Richard Cross, head of the emergency unit, claims that those taken to hospital have been very lucky to have escaped serious harm and appear, at this stage, to be suffering from only minor injuries. A special emergency phone line has been set up for enquiries relating to the accident. It is 3 9 9 9 4 3 3 3.

At present, traffic is being diverted to an alternative route. The boom gates are still down and the Greenhill Line is not open at present because there are quite a few problems in the area. Emergency transport workers are trying to repair a worn part of the track on the railway line which, at this stage, is believed to have caused the accident. Metropolitan transport officials claim that the line will be closed for up to six hours, so it's a good idea to avoid the area. There will be more details in the next traffic report before the six o'clock news.

ANNOUNCER: That is the end of this section. You now have half a minute to check the answers for Questions 1–7.

Listening skills PRACTICE 2 — TAPESCRIPT

ANNOUNCER: In a moment, you will hear a radio program presenter taking calls during a segment to help listeners find jobs. Three employers, John, Louise and Jamie, ring to talk about the vacancies they have in their workplaces.

Before you listen, look at Questions 8–13, which form part of a table. Note the example that has been done for you.

PROGRAM PRESENTER: It's ten to three and time for our employment segment today. We have three employers on the line ready to advertise vacancies in their workplaces. If you're interested, find a pen and paper and off we go. (*Pause*)

First on the line is John. Hello. Thank you for being part of our employment program. Tell us about the vacancy you have.

JOHN: Hello. I have a vacancy for a sales representative in the cosmetics field for work in the Southcity area. It's a casual position paying $140 per week. It involves two hours each day, Monday to Friday; that is, from six till eight in the evening.

PROGRAM PRESENTER: Well, thank you for that information … er … What experience would you expect the person to have?

JOHN: No formal qualifications would be necessary but we would expect the person to have some understanding of sales. It would be a good casual job for a college student.

PROGRAM PRESENTER: What number should we ring if we are interested?

JOHN: It's 3 double 5 6 double 7 9 2. I might add that the code is Q 3 4 9 7.

PROGRAM PRESENTER: What was that phone number again?

JOHN: It is 3 double 5 6 double 7 9 2.

PROGRAM PRESENTER: The next job that we have available is for a receptionist in the central business district … Louise, you've been holding on very patiently. First of all, would you be able to give me some details about the pay?

LOUISE: I'd really prefer to talk to the person about that.

PROGRAM PRESENTER: I must point out that on this program we need to give some idea of the salary to our listeners.

LOUISE: All right then, if it's necessary. We're looking at about … er … $400 a week.

PROGRAM PRESENTER: Okay, thanks for that. Would you be able to give me some more details please?

LOUISE: Yes, we're hoping that the person will have some computer skills and be able to type. He or she really needs to have done a word-processing course at the very least. We don't really care about receptionist training as we hope to train the person ourselves.

PROGRAM PRESENTER: And what about the phone number and the code then?

LOUISE: The number is 3 6 6 3 4 6 7 4 and the code is … Oh, I'm sorry, I don't seem to have it here.

PROGRAM PRESENTER: Never mind. We'll have to just give the phone number then. And now our final call for the program is for a baker in the Meeton area. The owner of the bakery is on the line. Hello Jamie, thanks for calling. Now, about the job then. Could you begin by telling us how much the weekly wage is?

JAMIE: It's usually $350 ... and more with overtime. Er ... about the job now ... Well, we don't need anyone with a lot of experience but we do expect that the person has at least completed an apprenticeship in the field. We really want the person to be keen and prepared to work hard.

PROGRAM PRESENTER: That sounds fair enough.

JAMIE: Yes, but the person has to be an early riser. We start baking at five in the morning.

PROGRAM PRESENTER: That's pretty early for most people. What time do you finish?

JAMIE: Normally about 1.00 p.m. unless there's overtime.

PROGRAM PRESENTER: Well, I'm afraid we still need the code and the phone number.

JAMIE: Okay the code first ... it's R 1 6 4 8 and the phone number is 3 8 4 2 7 4 7 3.

PROGRAM PRESENTER: Oh good, thanks then.

JAMIE: 'Bye.

PROGRAM PRESENTER: That's all we have time for today. I hope that we've been of assistance to all you listeners out there. We'll take some more calls tomorrow. It's time now for the 3 o'clock news.

ANNOUNCER: That is the end of this section. You now have half a minute to check the answers.

Skills for the Reading Module

One of the main difficulties experienced by students doing the Reading Module is not having enough time to complete the test. It is therefore essential to read both efficiently and effectively.

There are four main skills that you will need in order to do well in the IELTS Reading Module. It is useful to use the following procedure for each text that is given.

1. **Previewing** (about 2 minutes for each passage)
(a) Study the passage by noting:
- titles
- headings
- illustrations
- diagrams
- any print in bold type or italics.
(b) Study key parts of the passage by skimming. Read the first paragraph, which often focuses on the main idea. The first sentence of each paragraph usually expresses the key points of the paragraph. Generally, the concluding paragraph provides a summary of the given passage. You may wish to highlight these with a pen.

2. Interpreting the instructions and questions (about 2 minutes)

Read each word in the instructions carefully and ensure that you understand exactly what is required and in what form. For example, the instructions may say, 'Choose *no more than three words* from the passage for each answer'. In this situation, it would not be acceptable to write four or more words. Often students find the right answer but present it in the wrong form and, unfortunately, do not score any marks for that answer. Understanding what is required, therefore, is just as important as finding the right answer in the passage.

When you are looking at the questions, you need to recognise:

- what type of question you have to answer (is it gap-filling, multiple choice, matching information etc.?)

- whether the question requires a specific or a general answer

- what form the answer should take (is it a number, date, reason etc.?).

3. Scanning the text for specific answers (about 1 minute per question)

Use your time wisely. Spend no longer than one minute on finding each answer. Look only in the given text, table, diagram or graph for the answer required. Locate key words in the question and find them, or synonyms for them, in the text. The sentences around these words are most likely to contain the answers you need.

If you are still unsure of the answer after you have spent approximately one minute on the question, make a sensible guess in the appropriate form. You may wish to mark the answers you are unsure of in some way so that, if you do have time at the end of the Reading Module, you can check these answers again.

4. Checking your answers (about 3 minutes)

After you have completed your answers for each section, you need to check them. Check that you have followed the instructions exactly. If you have time, return to the answers you marked because you were unsure and decide if the answers you have given are the best ones.

Do not leave any answers blank as you do not lose marks for incorrect answers.

Helpful hints for the Practice Reading Module

- There may be some words in the passage with which you are unfamiliar. Use the strategies explained in the section 'Working out unfamiliar vocabulary' (see page 19) to help you work out the meanings of these words.

- Be aware of the use of connective words. These will help you with the general meaning of the text. If you are unsure of any answers, check the table of common connective words (see page 18).

- Note if there is a glossary accompanying the passage.

- Follow the instructions carefully. A correct response will be marked wrong if it is written in the wrong form.

Common connective words

Familiarity with these words would be useful in all IELTS test modules.

Common connective words indicating:

Addition	Sequence	Consequence	Contrast
in addition	first(ly)	as a result	however
and	initially	thus	on the other hand
similarly	second(ly) etc.	so	despite
likewise	to begin with	therefore	in spite of
as well as	then	consequently	though
besides	next	it follows that	although
furthermore	earlier/later	thereby	but
also	after this/that	eventually	on the contrary
moreover	following this/that	then	otherwise
and then	afterwards	in that case	yet
too		admittedly	instead of
not only ... but			rather
even			whereas
besides this/that			nonetheless

Certainty	Condition	Definition	even though
obviously	if	is	compared with
certainly	unless	refers to	in contrast
plainly	whether	means	alternatively
of course	provided that	that is	
undoubtedly	for	consists of	
	so that		
	whether		
	depending on		

Example	Reason	Time	Summary
for instance	since	before	in conclusion
one example	as	since	in summary
for example	so	as	lastly
just as	because (of)	until	finally
in particular	due to	meanwhile	to sum up
such as	owing to	at the moment	to conclude
namely	the reason why	when	to recapitulate
to illustrate	in other words	whenever	in short
	leads to	as soon as	
	cause	just as	

Working out unfamiliar vocabulary

When reading a passage in the IELTS test, it is most likely that you will come across words with which you are unfamiliar. Be prepared for this. You may not need to understand the exact meaning of an unknown word, unless there is a question directly related to it.

If you *do* need to know the meaning of an unfamiliar word, don't panic. There are various strategies that you can use to work out the meaning of the unknown words.

Check the context
Are there any clues in the surrounding words or phrases? Look particularly at the words just before and just after the unfamiliar words.

Look for a definition
Sometimes the writers realise that the word is an uncommon one so they define, restate, explain or give an example of it. Words that signal meaning often include 'is', 'means', 'refers to', 'that is', 'consists of'. For example, 'Snoring is a noise generated by vibrations of the soft parts of the throat during sleep.' The word 'is' signals a definition.

Remember, too, to check if there is a glossary.

Identify the word's place and purpose
Is it a noun, adjective, verb or adverb in the sentence? Are there any punctuation clues, for example semicolons or question marks?

Look for connective words
They are often near the unknown words and will usually help to identify the general direction of the argument, which will help to give some understanding of the unknown word. (Refer to page 18.)

Break the word down into syllables
Sometimes knowledge of common roots, affixes and possible similarity of words in your own language can help you to identify the meaning.

Treat the unknown word as an algebraic entity 'X'
Observe the relationship of the unknown word, 'X', to other words and concepts with which you are more familiar. Often this is enough to answer questions that include 'X'.

Practice for the Reading Module

To practise the skills required in the Reading Module, read the following passage entitled 'Astoria's private rental accommodation market' and complete Questions 1–20. (You may wish to photocopy and use the first 20 spaces of the answer sheet supplied on page 65.) Answers and explanations, including help on how to find the answers, are given after the questions, on pages 23–4.

(Suggested time: 35 minutes)

Astoria's private rental accommodation market

People spend time in private rental accommodation for a variety of reasons. The two most common ones are while waiting for public housing allocation and while saving to move on to home ownership. However, rental accommodation is losing its transitional status in Astoria. The percentage of long-term renters is increasing, as these people are unable to access public housing or home ownership.

Many studies have shown that discrimination on the basis of age, marital status, sex or race may affect some groups in their attempts to gain access to private rental housing. In practical terms, the significant costs associated with payments of a bond and rent in advance can be a barrier to access for lower income groups. Furthermore, many landlords and real estate agents believe that young single women, single mothers and women dependent on welfare benefits are unable to afford accommodation and, therefore, fail tenant selection criteria. Even though some of these women are not on low incomes, they experience discrimination. Single mothers face discrimination in greater numbers than any other group. Moreover, the rental problems faced by this group are generally worse in non-metropolitan areas.

There is a range of factors that affect the demand for private rental accommodation in Astoria. In the past, the 20–29 year age group has had the highest rental participation rates. A continued decline over the next decade in the size of this group indicates a long-term easing of demand. Other factors may also have an adverse effect on rental demand, such as falls in the rates of overseas immigration or high unemployment rates, especially among younger age groups. Furthermore, a decline in the participation in full-time employment of those in the 18–24 year age group will also have a negative influence on demand. On the other hand, a factor that may

reverse these trends will be the ongoing difficulties faced by low to moderate income groups in buying their own homes and the long waiting periods for public housing.

In Astoria, landlords play an important role as suppliers of housing in the private rental market. Generally, they fall into one of six categories. First, the *absentee landlord* is an individual who, rather than making a conscious investment decision, is forced to rent out his or her own home while away for a period of time. The absentee landlord typically holds no more than one property but, as a group, they control approximately 25 per cent of rental properties in Astoria.

The survey found that this group represents approximately 37 per cent of landlords. Next, the *equity investor* is the type of landlord who holds between two and four properties over many years with the intention of complete ownership to provide income in retirement. This group controls about 25 per cent of private rental properties. Similarly, the *negative gearer* owns a number of properties in the same range but for only a medium-term period. The investment is used to reduce overall taxation and the properties are generally sold when equity reaches 40–50 per cent. This type of investor controls approximately 20 per cent of all private rental properties. Another type of landlord is the *property speculator* who holds at least five properties and is always trying to increase the number. Property speculators generally own properties for a moderate to long period. Furthermore, they generate levels of equity equal to about 50 per cent of the value of their properties. The equity is then reinvested in additional properties. Rental income approximately equals costs. The *property manager* and the property speculator share equally 25 per cent of private rental properties in Astoria. The former type of landlord also has large numbers of properties but with equity levels three-quarters of the value of the properties. A property manager is typically an incorporated company whose main business is in the property field. The properties are held for long periods and the rental income generated significantly exceeds costs. The final category is that of the *casual landlord* who is typically a person who informally lets a room or shares the house he or she lives in, usually as a means of easing loan costs. Landlords in this group tend to own only the building they live in and are thought to make up the remaining share of the rental market.

A 1995 independent study on the characteristics of landlords in Astoria showed that their age tends to be slightly higher than the average age of the population. Sixty per cent of all landlords are male. This percentage actually increases with an increase in the number of properties owned by each individual. It was also found that 35 per cent of landlords are not in the paid work force owing to age. In addition, the study revealed that approximately 94 per cent of landlords own property in only one city and over half had owned rental property for more than ten years.

Glossary

dwelling: place of residence
equity: the value of a property owned by a person (such as a landlord) minus the amount of existing debt
bond: money paid by the tenant that is held as security for any damages that may occur

Questions 1–5

*Choose **ONE** phrase **A–I** from the list below to complete each key point. Write the appropriate letter **A–I** in boxes numbered **1–5** on your answer sheet. The information in the completed sentences should accurately reflect some of the points made by the writer.*

N.B.: There are more phrases A–I than sentences, so you will not use them all. You may use any phrase more than once.

1.   Demand for private rental accommodation . . .

2.   Access to home ownership . . .

3.   The requirement of paying rent in advance . . .

4.   The influence of decreased overseas immigration . . .

5.   The long wait for public housing . . .

A   . . . may become an obstacle for 30 per cent of renters.

B   . . . has the effect of sustaining demand for private rental accommodation.

C   . . . discriminates on the basis of race.

D   . . . is becoming less of a possibility for a growing percentage of renters.

E   . . . may result in less demand for private rental housing.

F   . . . results from high unemployment rates.

G   . . . prevents some people from obtaining accommodation.

H   . . . could fall in the future owing to the shrinking size of the 20–29 year age group.

I   . . . causes delays in access to home ownership.

Questions 6 and 7

USING NO MORE THAN THREE WORDS *for each, identify* **TWO** *types of women who regularly experience discrimination when seeking private rental accommodation. Write the names of one group each in boxes 6 and 7 on your answer sheet.*

6.   ....

7.   ....

Questions 8–13

Complete the table below. Choose a **NUMBER** *or* **NO MORE THAN THREE WORDS** *from the passage for each answer. Write your answers in boxes 8–13 on your answer sheet.*

Landlord type	Reason	Number of holdings	% of intended equity	Term of holdings	% of rental market
casual	easing loan costs	1	n/a*	n/a*	5
property speculator	further property purchase	5+	50	medium to long	... **(8)** ...
equity investor	... **(9)** ...	2–4	100	long	... **(10)** ...
property manager	corporate revenue	5+	... **(11)** ...	long	12.5
absentee landlord	away from home	1	n/a*	n/a*	25
negative gearer	reduce taxation	... **(12)** ...	40–50	... **(13)** ...	20

* information not available from reading passage

Questions 14–17

Do the following statements reflect the claims of the writer in the reading passage?

In boxes 14–17 on your answer sheet, write:
YES   *if the statement reflects the claims of the writer*
NO   *if the statement contradicts the writer's claims*
NOT GIVEN   *if it is impossible to say what the writer thinks about this.*

14.   Rural single mothers are more likely to encounter housing discrimination than their urban counterparts.

15.   A decrease in the rate of employment in the 18–24 year age group will have a positive effect on rental demand.

16. Landlords who are female tend to own fewer properties than male landlords.

17. Some 35 per cent of landlords do not hold a job and so survive only on income from their rental properties.

Questions 18–20

Choose the appropriate letters A–D and write them in boxes 18–20 on your answer sheet.

18. Single mothers on an average salary who rent ...

    A   would not be able to pay a bond and rent in advance.

    B   are likely to have access to public housing.

    C   are sometimes subjected to discrimination.

    D   usually receive welfare assistance.

19. The majority of landlords in Astoria ...

    A   own five or more properties.

    B   have not increased their wealth.

    C   no longer reside in the city

    D   have been landlords for over a decade.

20. The main purpose of the reading passage is ...

    A   to discuss issues and trends in private rental accommodation.

    B   to advise people who hope to become landlords.

    C   to suggest changes to private rental accommodation policy.

    D   to aid people who are looking for private rental accommodation.

Answers and explanations

1.   **H.** In the third paragraph it is stated that 'In the past, the 20–29 age group ... *A continued decline* over the next decade *in the size of this group* indicates *a long-term easing of demand.*'

2.   **D.** In the first paragraph it is stated that '... rental accommodation is *losing* its transitional status in Astoria. The percentage of long-term renters is *increasing*, as these people are *unable* to access public housing or *home ownership.*'

3.   **G.** In the second paragraph it is stated that '... the *significant costs* associated with payments of a bond and rent in advance can be *a barrier to access ...*'

4.   **E.** In the third paragraph it is stated that 'Other factors may also have *an adverse effect* on rental demand, such as *falls in the rates of overseas immigration ...*'

5.   **B.** In the third paragraph it is stated that 'On the other hand, a factor that may reverse *these trends* [referring to the negative influence on demand] will be the ongoing difficulties ... and the long waiting periods for public housing.'

6. and 7.   Any two of the following in any order: **young single women** OR **single mothers** OR **welfare dependent women**. Answers are in the second paragraph. Note that the question asked for TWO types of women. If you gave all three types, your answer is incorrect.

> To complete the table (Questions 8–13), refer to the fourth and fifth paragraphs, as all the information describing the landlord types is contained in these paragraphs. Note the topic sentence of the fourth paragraph.

8.   **12.5 per cent.** You are required to look beyond the particular category of 'property speculator'. The answer is found in the description of 'property manager'. 'The property manager *and* the property speculator *share equally 25 per cent* of private rental properties.' Therefore, the answer is *half of 25 per cent*, which is 12.5 per cent.

9.   **Income in retirement** OR **Complete ownership.** The key phrase is found in reference to the equity investor who has 'the intention of *complete ownership* to provide *income in retirement*'.

10.   **25 per cent.** The answer is found in reference to the equity investor. This group controls about '*25 per cent of private rental properties*'.

11.   **75 per cent.** The former type of landlord refers to the property manager, who has 'equity levels *three-quarters* of the value of the properties'. The category in the table requires the *percentage* intended equity so the answer must be in the form of a percentage. Three-quarters is the same as 75 per cent.

12.   **Two to four.** The answer is found in reference to the negative gearer who 'owns a number of properties *in the same range*'. The word 'similarly' connects 'negative gearer' to 'equity investor', who holds 'between two and four properties'.

13.   **Medium term.** This is found in reference to the negative gearer where it is stated that properties are held 'for only a *medium-term period*'.

14.   **Yes.** In the second paragraph it is stated that 'the rental problems faced by this group are generally *worse in non-metropolitan areas*'. 'Rural areas' is the same as 'non-metropolitan areas'.

15.   **No.** In the third paragraph it is stated that '*a decline in* the participation in *full-time employment* … will also have *a negative influence on demand*'.

16.   **Yes.** In the fifth paragraph it is stated that '*sixty per cent* of all landlords *are male. This percentage actually increases* with *an increase in the number of properties* owned by each individual'. Therefore, women tend to own fewer properties.

17.   **Not given.** In the sixth (last) paragraph it is stated that '35 per cent of landlords are *not in the paid work force …*', but there is no evidence for the second part of the statement. This group of landlords may receive income from other investments.

18.   **C.** In the second paragraph it is stated that 'Even though some of these women are *not on low incomes, they experience discrimination*'.

19.   **D.** In the sixth (last) paragraph it is stated that '*over half* had owned rental property for more than *ten years*'.

20.   **A.** The passage does not give advice, suggestions or help. It simply gives facts on private rental accommodation.

Skills for the Writing Module — Task 1

In Task 1 of the Writing Module, you are given about 20 minutes to write a minimum of 150 words. You are asked to look at a diagram, table, graph or short piece of text and describe the information in your own words. There are three important steps you should follow: preparation, writing and editing. These steps will help you to write a coherent and well-organised essay in the time given.

1. **Preparation** (about 2 minutes)
You need to spend 2–3 minutes working out exactly what you are going to do. You should pay attention to the following points:

- Study the question carefully. Most Task 1 writing involves writing a report that describes some information given. You may wish to note the instructions with a highlighting pen.
- Think carefully about the topic. Outline some pertinent points.
- Ensure that your ideas are arranged logically.

2. **Writing** (about 15 minutes)
When writing a Task 1 report, include:

- introductory sentence
- body paragraphs (1–3)
- concluding sentence (optional).

Introductory sentence
The introductory sentence explains what you are describing. For example:

> 'The table compares the population growth and interstate migration in each Australian state for 12 months to the end of 1994.'

> 'The graph shows the growth of computers in Australia between 1975 and 1995.'

> 'The pie chart represents the proportion of gases contained in natural gas.'

Using the column graph on page 28 as an example, you may choose to write, 'The column graph shows the percentage of men and women employed in several categories of executive positions in the ACME Oil Company between July 1993 and June 1994.'

Body paragraphs
When discussing the data presented in the task, identify significant trends and give examples that relate directly to the given information to support your statements. If you are explaining a process or an object and how it works, you need to group your information so that it follows a definite logical order. (A list of common sequential connectives can be found on page 18.)

Remember that the use of verbs expressed in the present passive voice is often appropriate when giving a description of a process or procedure. For example:

> 'Coffee beans *are pulped* to remove their casing. They *are* then *soaked* in water, *rinsed* thoroughly and *dried*. After the beans *are sorted*, they *are roasted* in a kiln and *blended*. Next, they *are packed* and *despatched* to shops and supermarkets.'

Concluding sentence (optional)
A simple concluding statement could include any of the following, where relevant:

- significant comments
- an overall summary of the ideas
- a potential solution
- future implications.

3. **Editing** (about 2 minutes)

Make sure that you have followed the instructions carefully. Be sure that you have written what you intended and that no important ideas are missing.

In the last few minutes, check for obvious errors, such as spelling or grammatical errors.

Describing graphs

Examples of phrases that may be used in describing a graph that illustrates past events are shown in the graph below.

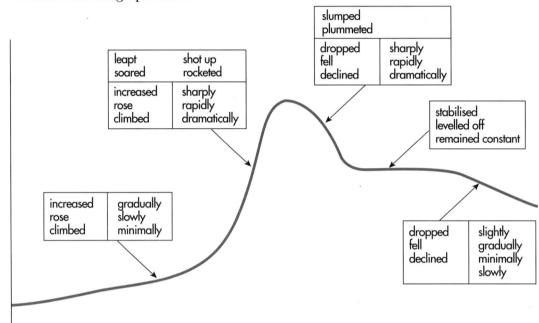

When discussing the future, the following expressions would be useful:

- ... is projected to rise sharply
- ... is forecast to drop slightly
- ... is expected to fall dramatically
- ... is predicted to decline steadily.

 # Practice for the Writing Module — Task 1

Line graphs

When describing information in a **line graph** it is important to look at significant patterns and trends. You need to ask yourself questions that are relevant to these trends. The following steps will help you to do the Practice Writing Task 1 on page 27.

1. What relationship and projections does figure 1 show?

2. Comment on the trends relating to energy demand. (Use appropriate phrases from the model graph above and examples with the years and units of energy to support your statements.)

3. Comment on the energy available from fossil fuels. (Support your comments in the same way as explained in point 2 above.)

4. Comment on the excess energy. Why do you think that Freedonia had more energy than it needed?

5. Comment on the energy gap. Can you offer a solution?

A model answer in the form of a report is given on page 27. The useful phrases that were noted in the graph and text above have been italicised in this model report.

You should spend about 20 minutes on this task.

The graph (figure 1) shows the demand for energy and the energy available from fossil fuels in Freedonia from 1985 to 2005.

Write a report for a university lecturer describing the information shown in the graph.

You should write at least 150 words.

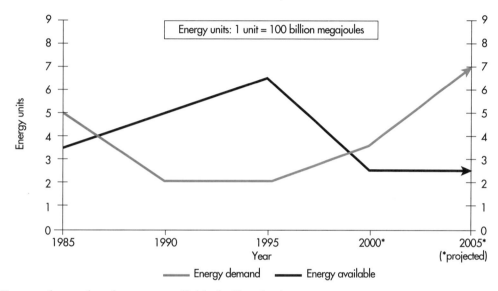

Figure 1: Energy demand and energy available in Freedonia

Model answer: describing information in a line graph

Figure 1 shows the relationship between demand for energy and the energy available from fossil fuels in Freedonia since 1985 and gives projections to the year 2005. The energy in the graph is measured in units each of which is equivalent to 100 billion megajoules.

The demand for energy *dropped steadily between 1985 and 1990* from 5 units of energy to approximately 2 units. From 1990 until about 1995, energy demand appeared to *level off and remained constant* at about 2 units of energy. From this time onwards, energy demand *climbs dramatically* from 2 units of energy in 1996 and is projected to reach 7 units in the year 2005. Furthermore, the forecast is for energy demand to *continue to rise* in the future.

In contrast, the amount of energy available from fossil fuels *increased quite rapidly* from about 3.5 units in 1985 until it *reached a peak* of 6.5 in 1995. From this point onwards it is *projected to decline dramatically* until *it remains constant* at an availability level of around 2.5 units from the year 2000.

The energy demand and energy available from fossil fuels resulted in an excess amount of energy available in the 1990s in Freedonia, which perhaps was due to the availability of alternative sources of energy. On the other hand, an energy gap that continues to widen is forecast, beginning in the late 1990s. In the future, Freedonians will have to enforce energy saving measures or look towards the use of alternative sources of energy.

(Approximately 220 words)

Column graphs

When describing information in a **column graph**, it is important, as with line graphs, to look for significant trends but also to make comparisons between categories. Another Practice Writing Task 1 is given below. Consider the following questions. They should help you to identify some points for discussion in writing the report on the graph that we have called figure 2.

- Introductory sentence. What is the graph examining?
- In which job category are women most represented?
- In which job category are men least represented?
- Which job category shows the least difference between the percentage of men and women employed?
- What is the overall trend shown in the graph?
- Concluding sentence. What does this trend mean? Is there a solution to the potential problem?

After you have written the Task 1 essay on the column graph, look at the model answer on page 29, which highlights some important elements.

You should spend about 20 minutes on this task.

The graph (figure 2) shows the percentage of men and women employed in executive positions in ACME Oil Company from July 1993 to June 1994.

Write a report for a university lecturer describing the information shown in the graph.

You should write at least 150 words.

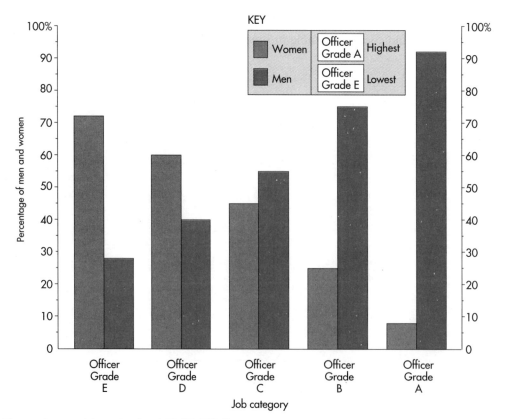

Figure 2: Executive positions in the ACME Oil Company

Model answer: describing information in a column graph

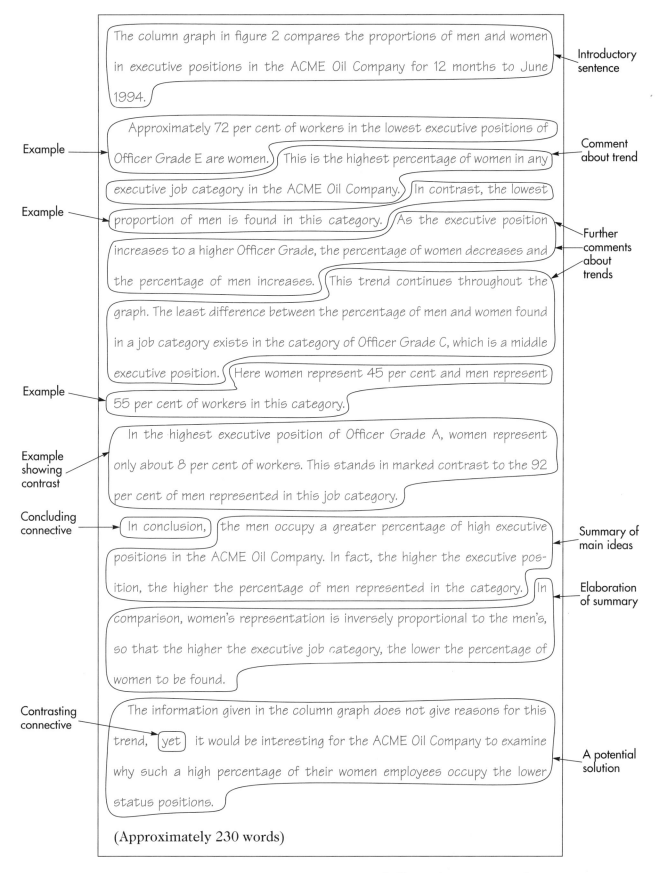

Introductory sentence

The column graph in figure 2 compares the proportions of men and women in executive positions in the ACME Oil Company for 12 months to June 1994.

Example

Approximately 72 per cent of workers in the lowest executive positions of Officer Grade E are women.

Comment about trend

This is the highest percentage of women in any executive job category in the ACME Oil Company.

Example

In contrast, the lowest proportion of men is found in this category.

Further comments about trends

As the executive position increases to a higher Officer Grade, the percentage of women decreases and the percentage of men increases. This trend continues throughout the graph. The least difference between the percentage of men and women found in a job category exists in the category of Officer Grade C, which is a middle executive position.

Example

Here women represent 45 per cent and men represent 55 per cent of workers in this category.

Example showing contrast

In the highest executive position of Officer Grade A, women represent only about 8 per cent of workers. This stands in marked contrast to the 92 per cent of men represented in this job category.

Concluding connective

In conclusion,

Summary of main ideas

the men occupy a greater percentage of high executive positions in the ACME Oil Company. In fact, the higher the executive position, the higher the percentage of men represented in the category.

Elaboration of summary

In comparison, women's representation is inversely proportional to the men's, so that the higher the executive job category, the lower the percentage of women to be found.

Contrasting connective

The information given in the column graph does not give reasons for this trend, yet it would be interesting for the ACME Oil Company to examine why such a high percentage of their women employees occupy the lower status positions.

A potential solution

(Approximately 230 words)

Skills for the Writing Module — Task 2

All too often students begin planning or even writing their answers in the IELTS Writing Module before they understand what is actually expected of them. Following the steps below will help you to plan a well-structured and coherent essay or report that addresses the given task.

1. Preparation

You may wish to spend about 5–7 minutes working out exactly what you are going to do. There are five steps to consider:

- Study the question carefully. Most task statements or questions have a key instructional word or words telling you what to do. Note these words with a highlighting pen.

    There are also key topic words that point to the most important parts of the question. Underline those words too. Ask yourself how the key words relate to the given instruction.

- Think carefully about the topic. How do you feel about it?

- Establish a point of view and list some points for development. The answer normally takes the form of a short essay. The word 'essay' comes from the French verb *essayer*, which means 'to attempt or try out' or 'to test'. In an IELTS Writing Module Task 2 answer, your purpose is to develop your point of view in a convincing way.

- Decide which points will be written as topic sentences. Think about how they will develop into paragraphs.

- Ensure that your points are arranged in a logical order.

2. Writing

When you are writing a Task 2 answer, a structure based on the following elements could be used (summarised in the flow chart opposite).

Introductory paragraph

The introduction of a Task 2 answer should begin with a general statement or idea of your own that takes into account the key topic words or their synonyms. The last sentence of the introduction should include a thesis statement, which shows the point of view or direction that will be taken in the answer.

Body paragraphs

Body paragraphs each consist of several sentences that are arranged in a logical way to develop a main idea. You can expect to write about 2–4 body paragraphs for a Task 2 answer. Each of these contains an appropriate connective word to ensure a smooth transition between paragraphs. (See page 18 for a list of common connective words.) This connective is then put in a topic sentence, which is the main point of the paragraph clearly stated in a sentence. Every sentence in the paragraph must be directly related to it. Try to develop every paragraph adequately. This may be done through the use of examples, explanations, detail, logical inference, cause and effect, or making comparisons or contrasts. There are many different ways to organise your ideas for body paragraphs. Be confident of the ideas you choose.

The conclusion

A good conclusion serves several purposes:

- It indicates the end of your essay. (For use of concluding connectives, see page 18.)
- It gives your final thoughts and assessments on the essay subject.
- It weighs up the points in your essay and should strengthen your thesis statement.

Do not simply repeat your opening paragraph. This appears too mechanical and superficial.

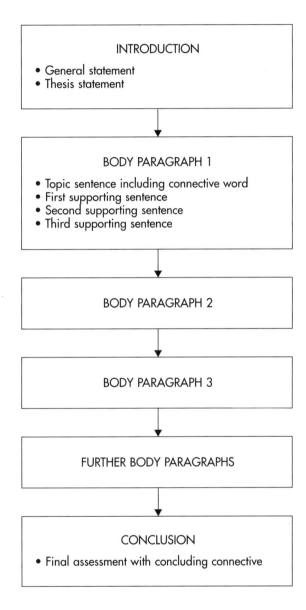

3. **Editing** (about 3–5 minutes)

In the last few minutes, you should check for obvious errors, such as spelling or grammatical errors. Be sure that you have written what you intended and that there are no important ideas missing.

Study the checklist for editing on page 32. It lists points to think about when checking your essay. Become familiar with the list so that you will know what to check for in the actual IELTS Writing Module.

Checklist for editing

1. ____ I have used accurate grammatical structures, for example consistent verb tenses, subject–verb agreement, accurate word formation (especially of nouns, verbs and adjectives) and appropriate use of 'a' and 'the' as well as prepositions.

2. ____ I have used a range of sentence structures.

3. ____ I have used appropriate vocabulary.

4. ____ I have used accurate spelling.

5. ____ I have stated the main idea for each paragraph in a topic sentence and all the points are related to this topic.

6. ____ I have used connective words effectively to link ideas so that the thoughts move logically and clearly from sentence to sentence and paragraph to paragraph.

7. ____ I have developed each paragraph adequately.

8. ____ I have supplied enough detailed information and sufficient examples or facts.

9. ____ I have developed a definite point of view.

10. ____ Every paragraph that I have written has definitely helped to address the task.

 # Practice for the Writing Module — Task 2

Carry out the following Practice Writing Task 2, which asks for comment and opinion on a given statement. Afterwards, study the model answer that follows it and notice:

- the use of connective words (in italics)

- the use of pronouns: they, he, she, it, these, their

- the repetition of key words and their synonyms, such as examination/assessment, unfair/inaccurate

- the use of topic sentences

- how the thesis statement shows the point of view that is later developed in the answer

- the expansion of body paragraphs through the use of explanations, examples and contrasting viewpoints

- the strengthening of the thesis statement in the conclusion.

When you are writing your answer, try to use some of these devices to help you write coherently.

You should spend about 40 minutes on this task.

Present a written argument or case to an educated non-specialist audience on the following topic.

'In the last 20 years, the assessment of students has undergone major transformation. Many educational institutions no longer use formal examinations as a means of assessment as they believe formal examination results are an unfair indication of a student's ability.'

To what extent do you agree or disagree with this statement?

Give reasons for your answer.

You should write at least 250 words.

You should use your own ideas, knowledge and experience and support your arguments with examples and relevant evidence.

Model Task 2 answer

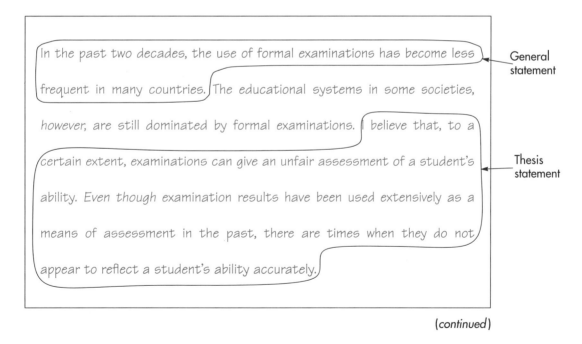

In the past two decades, the use of formal examinations has become less frequent in many countries. The educational systems in some societies, however, are still dominated by formal examinations. I believe that, to a certain extent, examinations can give an unfair assessment of a student's ability. Even though examination results have been used extensively as a means of assessment in the past, there are times when they do not appear to reflect a student's ability accurately.

General statement

Thesis statement

(continued)

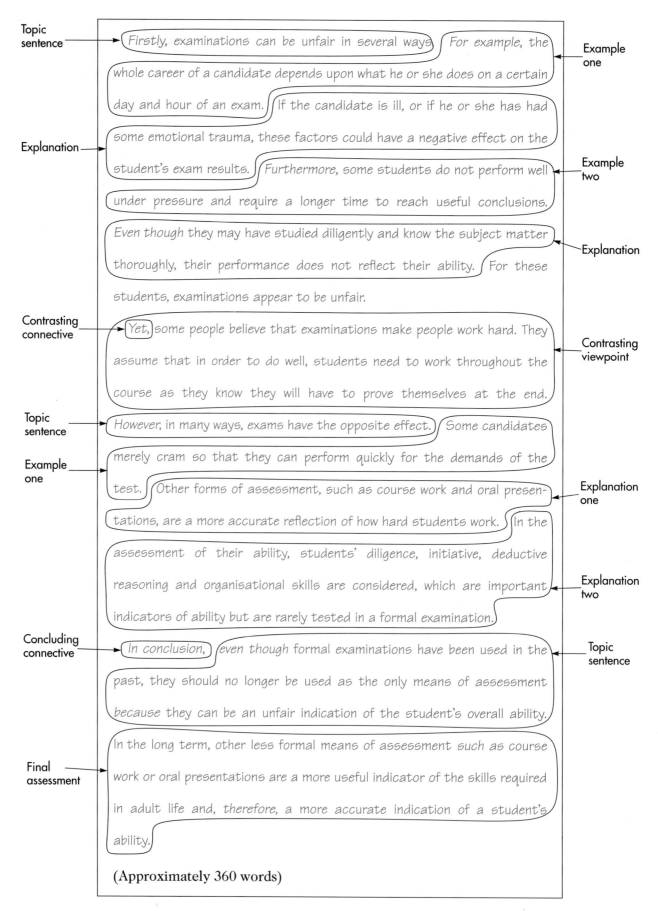

Topic sentence → *Firstly, examinations can be unfair in several ways.*

Example one → *For example, the whole career of a candidate depends upon what he or she does on a certain day and hour of an exam.*

Explanation → *If the candidate is ill, or if he or she has had some emotional trauma, these factors could have a negative effect on the student's exam results.*

Example two → *Furthermore, some students do not perform well under pressure and require a longer time to reach useful conclusions.*

Explanation → *Even though they may have studied diligently and know the subject matter thoroughly, their performance does not reflect their ability. For these students, examinations appear to be unfair.*

Contrasting connective → *Yet,*

Contrasting viewpoint → *some people believe that examinations make people work hard. They assume that in order to do well, students need to work throughout the course as they know they will have to prove themselves at the end.*

Topic sentence → *However, in many ways, exams have the opposite effect.*

Example one → *Some candidates merely cram so that they can perform quickly for the demands of the test.*

Explanation one → *Other forms of assessment, such as course work and oral presentations, are a more accurate reflection of how hard students work.*

Explanation two → *In the assessment of their ability, students' diligence, initiative, deductive reasoning and organisational skills are considered, which are important indicators of ability but are rarely tested in a formal examination.*

Concluding connective → *In conclusion,*

Topic sentence → *even though formal examinations have been used in the past, they should no longer be used as the only means of assessment because they can be an unfair indication of the student's overall ability.*

Final assessment → *In the long term, other less formal means of assessment such as course work or oral presentations are a more useful indicator of the skills required in adult life and, therefore, a more accurate indication of a student's ability.*

(Approximately 360 words)

Skills for the Speaking Module

For security reasons you will be asked to bring your passport or some other form of photographic identification. You will be asked to sign your name, which will be matched up with the photograph and signature on your IELTS application form.

The test will be conducted in three parts, which will be described in turn.

PART 1: Introduction and interview

In the introduction of Part 1, the examiner will first greet you and then introduce himself or herself and will invite you to do the same. Your identification will also be checked here.

SKILL Greeting the interviewer and introducing yourself.

Phrases you could use:

> • 'Good afternoon. My name is ＿＿(name).'
>
> • 'Hello. My name is ＿＿(name)＿＿ but most of my friends call me ＿＿(shortened version of name/nickname).'

The interview section of Part 1 will follow with questions related closely to your own personal life and then continue with further questions that are related to your wider experience. Initially you may be asked about your background or your home or what you are currently doing. The questions may extend to topics related to your country, such as customs or lifestyles and your personal involvement with these.

The aim of this Part 1 interview is to show that you can answer the specific questions that the interviewer asks. There are two main skills that you need to practise for this part of the test:

• You will need to give relevant factual information related to yourself.

• You will also need to be able to express your opinions or your attitudes towards a familiar issue without relying on the interviewer to help you.

The idea is for you to talk and give as much information as you can. Even if you are not sure what the interviewer is asking you, do your best to give an answer. Do not simply answer 'yes' or 'no'. Do not, however, memorise responses. If you appear to be reciting from memory, the examiner will disregard what you are saying.

Before you begin preparing for the interview section of Part 1, you may wish to make a list of topics related to your country, culture, lifestyle, personal interests etc. Once you have completed such a list, think about possible questions you could be asked that relate to the skills for this part of the test. You can gain further practice by answering questions you could be asked from the task cards on the following pages.

With a partner, practise interviewing and being interviewed. Try to give full and comprehensive answers to each question and include some of the useful phrases given in this part.

Questions you may be asked:

The place in which you grew up

- Could you describe your home city/town/village?
- What would a tourist go to see there?
- How do people your age spend their weekends in your home city/town/village?
- Do you enjoy living there? [Why?]

OR

Work

- Where do you work?
- How do you get there?
- What does an average day at work involve?
- How did you become interested in the type of work you do?
- Are there things you would like to change about your work?

OR

Study

- What are you studying at the moment?
- When did you decide to study these subjects?
- What influenced you to make this decision?
- Do you enjoy studying these subjects?
- How will they help you with your future career?

THEN

Family

- Tell me about your family members.
- Where do they live?
- What is each person doing at present?
- Are there special times in the year that you spend together?
- Do you socialise with them at other times?

OR

Studying English

- When did you first start learning English?
- Which English skill do you find easiest to learn? Why?
- In what ways do you practise your English?
- How will improving your English benefit you personally?

OR

Transport

- What public transport is available in your home town?
- How much do fares cost?
- Are there any discounts for students?
- What hours does public transport operate?
- Is it a system that you would recommend to others? (Why?)

OR

Questions about some other familiar topic.

Phrases you could use

when giving factual information:	when commenting:
Generally	Now, let me see
Usually	Surprisingly enough
Most of the time	Actually
On the whole	Interestingly enough

Phrases you could use to introduce your own opinion:

In my opinion	Well, personally speaking
I personally think	It seems that
I believe that	From my point of view
I feel that	As I see it
To my mind	I'm quite convinced that
Obviously	I'm fairly certain that

PART 2: Individual long turn

In Part 2, the examiner wants you to have a long turn speaking on your own that lasts between one and two minutes.

You will be given spare paper and a pencil as well as a topic written on a task card. On this task card will be written a general instruction related to the given topic and several suggestions of what you should include in your long turn. You will also be given a minute to think about and/or make some notes on what you are going to say. The examiner will tell you when to begin. Speak as clearly as you can, and try to present your ideas in a logical way. If you speak for more than two minutes, the examiner will ask you to finish. Then you may be asked some further questions before the examiner begins the discussion in Part 3.

In Part 2, the topics will be reasonably easy to talk about. You can prepare for this part by choosing simple topics such as a favourite book, or a film or television program, a special friend, or even a type of animal you like. Make notes about what you would like to say. Study the suggestions for useful phrases in this part to help you organise your speech. Then present your ideas to a partner. Even if you feel that you do not have very much to say about a topic, try to keep talking. Practise speaking for up to two minutes. For further practice, select one of the Practice Task Cards. Study the suggestions about what you should say and give yourself one minute to prepare and jot down ideas before presenting your ideas to a partner.

Practice Task Card A

Describe a famous person whom you admire.

You should say:
- who this person is
- what he or she is like
- the length of time you have admired this person
- for what this person is well known

and explain the reason why you look up to this person.

Task A follow-up questions:
Do you have friends or family who also look up to this person?
Do you think that you will continue to admire this person in the future?

Practice Task Card B

> Describe a place that is very special to you.
>
> You should say:
> - where it is
> - what it is like there
> - how often you go there
> - how you feel when you are there
>
> and explain why this place is important to you.

Task B follow-up questions:
Is this place also significant for anyone else?
Do you think that you will always consider it special?

Phrases you could use to begin Part 2:

> To start with
> I would like to begin with
> I would like to tell you about

In Part 2, your sentences will need to follow logically, so the ideas need to be organised using appropriate connective words and phrases such as:

so	although
next	however
also	not only ... but
besides this	on the other hand
as well as	yet
and then	otherwise
perhaps I should mention	what's more
afterwards	though

Phrases you could use when giving examples:

For instance	For one thing
Take the way	To give you an idea
Take for example	namely

Phrases you could use to complete Part 2:

So, in the end	Finally
So,	To finish off
All in all	I'd like to finish with

PART 3: Two-way discussion

In Part 3, the interviewer will converse with you in greater depth on a particular, more abstract topic. This two-way discussion will be linked by theme to the topic you spoke about in Part 2.

During this part, the interviewer will allow this discussion to become more complex by asking you a series of questions. You may have to give answers that describe, compare, evaluate, justify or speculate on ideas related broadly to an issue.

In order to prepare for Part 3, select one of the Practice Task Cards and ask a partner to discuss the given question suggestions with you. Try also to think of further topics that may be included. In your discussion answers, try to include some of the suggestions for useful phrases related to the skills required for the two-way discussion.

Practice related to Task Card A

Wealth
- (comment on) the wealth of famous people
- (compare) the differences in the way celebrities spend their money
- (justify or otherwise) the amount of money famous people earn

Marketing
- (describe) the role marketing plays in famous people's lives
- (justify or otherwise) the necessity of marketing in the lives of famous people
- (evaluate) the worth of marketing in famous people's lives

The Press
- (describe) the responsibilities they have to report about famous people's lives
- (justify or otherwise) the reporting of very private details about celebrities
- (evaluate) the press's power to positively or negatively influence readers towards famous people

Practice related to Task Card B

The City
- (describe) the advantages related to city living
- (compare) the main differences between country and city living
- (justify) where you prefer to live

Population Growth
- (comment on) the current population in your home town/city
- (explain) the changes in population growth over the past 20 years
- (speculate on) the future trend of population growth

Urbanisation
- (describe) the hazards of urbanisation
- (justify) the reason why people move from country to city areas
- (speculate) on the effects of megacities of the future

Useful phrases for Part 3

Phrases you could use when comparing and contrasting:

The main difference	just a little different
One of the differences	totally different
In contrast/on the other hand	slightly different
Similarly/likewise	Whereas/while

Phrases you could use when speculating:

It may/could/might (well) be that	Maybe
It's quite possible that	I guess
I imagine that	I suppose
Perhaps	I expect

Phrases you could use when justifying:

that's why	you see
besides	to be honest
because	let me explain
so	the reason why
what I mean is	what I'm saying is

Phrases you could use to give yourself time to think in the discussion:

Now, let me think	The best way I can answer this is
It's difficult to say exactly, but	Mm, that's a difficult question. Let me see
That's an interesting question	I'll have to think about that
How shall I put it?	Let's put it this way

Assessment

The assessment will be based on your average performance over the three parts of the test. Your speaking skills as a whole will be marked on four separate scales.

Fluency and coherence: Do you express your ideas clearly and logically at a normal rate and without long hesitations?

Lexical resource: Do you use a wide range of vocabulary that is appropriate?

Grammatical range and accuracy: Do you use a variety of grammatical structures in your speech and make only a few minor errors?

Pronunciation: Are you easy to understand? Does your English pronunciation sound natural?

Each of these categories will be awarded a score and these scores will be averaged to provide a final band score for the Speaking Module.

Speaking test hints

Try to improve your pronunciation, intonation and fluency. One way to do this is to listen to native speakers in a variety of situations such as on radio news. Record several news items, listen to them and try to imitate the speaker's pronunciation, intonation and fluency.

Try to improve your grammar. Common errors in speech often include verb formations, especially agreements and tenses as well as article and prepositional errors. Learn the appropriate grammatical rules for these and try to implement them naturally when you speak.

Try to improve your vocabulary. In the first two parts of the test, the examiner cannot explain any vocabulary that you do not understand, so your vocabulary needs to be quite extensive. Make a commitment to increase your vocabulary every day. Flash cards, with new words written on one side and their meaning on the reverse, are one very useful technique you could use. Try to incorporate these new words into your current spoken vocabulary. Include words and phrases that native speakers use, such as idioms and phrasal verbs. Ensure that you understand how to use connective words and discourse markers appropriately so that your ideas follow logically and coherently.

Remember that the examiner will consider the combination of all these communication skills for assessment.

 # IELTS study hints

The following study hints will help you in the weeks leading up to the IELTS.
- Become familiar with the test as early as possible. The skills being tested in the IELTS take time to build up. Cramming is not an effective study technique for IELTS.
- Use your study time efficiently. Study when you are fresh and after you have planned a timetable, make sure that you keep to it. Set goals and ensure that you have adequate breaks. In the IELTS test, each of the four Band Modules — Listening, Reading, Writing and Speaking — carries the same weight. Study each skill carefully and spend more time on the skills in which you feel you are weak.
- Be aware of the exact procedure for the test. Be very clear on the order of each section, its length and the specific question types. (See pages 1–5 for information on test procedure.) There are many resources available to help you practise these skills.
- Having a study partner or a study group is an excellent idea. Other students may raise issues that you have not considered.
- Seek help from teachers, friends and native English speakers.

 # Countdown to the test

Days before the test

This is not a time for intensive study. It is a time to review skills and your test technique. It is important to exercise, eat, rest and sleep well during the week in which you will take the test.

Leave nothing to chance. If you do not know how to get to the test centre, try going there at a similar time one or two weeks before the real test.

The night before the test

You must have a good dinner and go to bed at your normal time — not too early and not too late, as you do not want to disrupt your sleep pattern if possible.

Have everything ready that you need to take with you to the test so you can simply pick it up in the morning, for example the test registration form, passport, test number, pens, pencils, erasers etc. A pen that runs dry or a pencil that breaks can take several minutes to replace. Check before the exam exactly what articles you need. Set your alarm clock the night before or arrange a wake-up call.

On the morning of the test

Eat a good breakfast. You will have several hours of concentration ahead of you and you will need food and drink in the morning. You may even want to bring more food or a snack with you, especially if your speaking test is at a later time that day. You cannot, however, take food or drink into the exam room. If possible, wear a watch in case you cannot see the clock in the exam room. It is essential that you keep track of time.

Give yourself plenty of time to get to the test centre. You will be required to complete a registration form and to show your passport before you enter the examination room so you must arrive at the time specified by your test centre. If you are early, you could go for a walk. If you are late, you will not be allowed to enter. Avoid the added tension of having to rush.

During the test

Most students at the test will feel nervous. This is quite normal. In fact, it can actually be quite helpful in terms of motivation. It may make you alert and help you to focus. The aim is for you to try to perform at your optimum level.

In contrast, high levels of anxiety can affect a student's performance. However, much of this anxiety can be overcome by good preparation, familiarity with test details and a positive attitude.

The examination room should be suitable for testing — that is, the lighting, ventilation and temperature should be appropriate. If you are uncomfortable because of any of these factors or if there is some other problem, such as not being able to hear the recording of the Listening Module, make sure you ask the person in charge to do something about it. For example, you may ask to change seats.

Examination technique

By using good examination technique you could help to improve your overall score for the IELTS test.

Remember that every section is marked independently. Do not jeopardise your performance in one section just because you believe that you have done badly in another. Do not underestimate or try to predict your outcome. You may, in fact, have done better than you imagined.

Focus on what you know rather than on what you don't know while you are doing the test.

Ensure that you adhere to the times suggested, as they usually correspond to the number of marks given for a particular question.

In the Listening and Reading Modules, it is a good idea to write down an answer, even if you are not sure of it, before moving on to the next question. Many students intend to return to the answers they have omitted at the end of the test but do not have enough time to do so. Furthermore, by writing your best answer at the actual time of reading the question, you save the time you need to spend again on re-reading the question and re-acquainting yourself with the subject matter. If you are not confident about your answer, mark it in some way and return to it at the end.

Do not leave any answers blank. You are not penalised for incorrect answers, so 'guess' wisely.

Practice Listening *Papers*

The three Practice Listening Papers that follow should be attempted under test conditions. The Listening passages can be found on the audio tape cassettes, as specified below. The tape should be played once only and no dictionary or other reference book may be used.

As in the real IELTS test, it is suggested that you write your answers directly onto the pages of the question paper. Alternatively, use a separate piece of paper for your answers. (In the actual test, you will be given time to transfer your answers onto an answer sheet. This is not necessary for the purposes of these Practice Papers.)

You may check your answers on pages 143–4. Tapescripts are also provided for later reference on pages 154–76.

Practice Listening Paper 1 (pages 44–50)	Audio Cassette One, Side B
Practice Listening Paper 2 (pages 51–6)	Audio Cassette Two, Side A
Practice Listening Paper 3 (pages 57–63)	Audio Cassette Two, Side B

IELTS Practice Listening Subtest

PAPER ONE

TIME ALLOWED: 30 minutes

NUMBER OF QUESTIONS: 41

Audio Cassette One, Side B

Instructions

- *This is a test to see how well you understand spoken English.*

- *You will hear several different recordings and you will have to answer questions on what you hear.*

- *The test is divided into four sections.*

- *There will be time for you to read the instructions and questions, and you will have a chance to check your work.*

- *You will hear each recording once only.*

- *(At the end of the real IELTS test, you will have ten minutes to transfer your answers to an answer sheet.)*

- *Now move on to Section 1 on the next page.*

Section 1   Questions 1–11

Questions 1–3

Circle the correct answer.

1. Claudia and Toshio decide to go to . . .

   A   the coast.   **C**   the desert.

   B   Sydney.   **D**   the mountains.

2. Toshio doesn't like . . .

   A   setting up tents.   **C**   sleeping outdoors.

   B   campfires.   **D**   cooking outdoors.

3. Claudia doesn't like youth hostels because . . .

   A   she dislikes meeting people.   **C**   there's no privacy.

   B   the beds are uncomfortable.   **D**   the kitchens are unfamiliar.

Questions 4–7

Tick (✓) in the appropriate column. Where necessary, write **NO MORE THAN TWO WORDS**.

Who will join Claudia and Toshio?

Question	Name	Will join	Will NOT join,	going to . . .
	Peter		*Example* ✓	Hong Kong
(4)	Maria			
	Gyorg	*Example* ✓		
(5)	David Wong			
(6)	Walter Wong			
(7)	Jennifer			
	Michael Sullivan		✓	Stay home

Questions 8–11

Complete the form below by filling in the blanks.

How does Toshio fill out the form?

<table>
<tr>
<td colspan="2" align="center"><h1>Sunnystones Holiday Rental Agency</h1> Rental Application Form </td>
</tr>
<tr>
<td align="center"><u>Applicant #1</u></td>
<td align="center"><u>Applicant #2</u></td>
</tr>
<tr>
<td>Name: Toshio Jones</td>
<td>Name: Claudia Hussein</td>
</tr>
<tr>
<td>Address: 52 Miller St
Chapmanville</td>
<td>Address: (Question 8)
614 .... St
Chapmanville</td>
</tr>
<tr>
<td>Phone: 3545 6681</td>
<td>Phone: 3543 2349</td>
</tr>
<tr>
<td colspan="2">(Question 9)
Credit card number: ....</td>
</tr>
<tr>
<td colspan="2">(Question 10)
Credit card type: ....</td>
</tr>
<tr>
<td colspan="2">(Question 11)
Deposit amount: $..</td>
</tr>
</table>

Section 2   *Questions 12–21*

Questions 12 and 13

Choose the letters corresponding to the correct people.

12.   Which person is Bruce Chandler?   13.   Which person is Donna Wilcox?

Question 14

*Circle the letter **A–D** indicating the location of the speaker.*

14.   Where is Jennifer Davis (the speaker)?

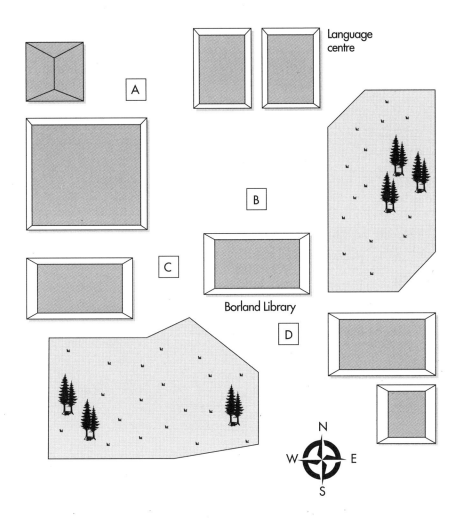

Questions 15 and 16

*Write a **NUMBER** for each answer.*

15.   The Maslow University campus has .... buildings.

16.   The buildings are on .... hectares of land.

Questions 17–19

Circle the correct answer.

17.   Before immigrating, John Maslow was . . .

           A   a teacher.   **C**   a college president.

           B   a trainer.   **D**   a mathematician.

18.   Maslow's Teacher's College ...

              A   operated for 10 years.   **C**   closed in 1848.

              B   was originally a private college.   **D**   trained high-school teachers.

19.   Maslow University ...

              A   is 11 kilometres from the city centre.   **C**   was established after Riversdale University.

              B   was established in 1866.   **D**   was built next to Maslow Teacher's College.

Questions 20 and 21

*Circle **TWO** letters.*

20–21. Riversdale University normally beats Maslow University at ...

              A   basketball.

              B   women's swimming.

              C   soccer.

              D   track and field.

              E   baseball.

              F   men's swimming.

              G   football.

Section 3   *Questions 22–33*

Questions 22 and 23

*Complete the notes below. Write **NO MORE THAN TWO WORDS** or **NUMBERS** for each answer.*

NOTES ON COFFEE

	Example • Journal: Food Economics Review
22.	• Coffee farming provides work for .... people.
	• Great economic importance
23.	• Ranked .... most important commodity in world
	• Most farmers produce coffee on 4–5 hectares of land.

Questions 24–27

Complete the table.

COFFEE BEAN TYPE	GROWING ALTITUDE	USED FOR	LARGEST GROWER COUNTRY
Arabica	*Example* 600–2000 metres	*Example* premium coffee	*Example* Brazil
Robusta	(24)	(25)	(27) ......
Liberica	*Example* below 1200 metres	(26)	

Questions 28–30

Tick (√) the relevant box for each country.

Country	Style of coffee preferred		
	(28) Instant coffee	(29) Espresso coffee	(30) Brewed coffee
Brazil			
France			
Germany			
Italy			
Japan			
Norway			√ *Example*
Sweden			√ *Example*
USA			
UK			

Questions 31–33

*Complete the sentences below. Write **NO MORE THAN THREE WORDS** for each answer.*

31. The ICO was established by ....

32. .... destroyed the 1975 Brazil coffee crop.

Circle the correct answer.

33. Because of the Brazil coffee crop failure, ...

A	the ICO had to supply the world coffee market.	**C**	prices remained high.
B	prices rose, then fell.	**D**	premium coffee became unavailable.

Section 4   *Questions 34–41*

Questions 34 and 35

Write **NO MORE THAN ONE WORD** for each answer.

What is the main interest in a meeting...

34. for the meeting leader? ....

35. for the facilitator? ....

Questions 36–41

*Complete the table below by writing the appropriate letter **A–E** in each blank box.*

Link each task below to the appropriate global responsibility.

Facilitator's global responsibilities

'Blueprinting'	=	**A**
'Pro-integration'	=	**B**
'Focusing'	=	**C**
'Prompting'	=	**D**
'Friction management'	=	**E**

Tasks

writing an agenda	*Example* A
defining technical terms	**(36)** ....
maintaining harmony	**(37)** ....
getting to know participants	**(38)** ....
guiding discussion	**(39)** ....
promoting agreement	**(40)** ....
encouraging everyone's participation	**(41)** ....

IELTS Practice Listening Subtest

PAPER TWO

LENGTH OF TIME: 30 minutes
NUMBER OF QUESTIONS: 42

Audio Cassette Two, Side A

Instructions

- *This is a test to see how well you understand spoken English.*

- *You will hear several different recordings and you will have to answer questions on what you hear.*

- *The test is divided into four sections.*

- *There will be time for you to read the instructions and questions, and you will have a chance to check your work.*

- *You will hear each recording once only.*

- *(At the end of the real IELTS test, you will have ten minutes to transfer your answers to an answer sheet.)*

- *Now turn to Section 1 on the next page.*

Section 1   *Questions 1–11*

Questions 1 and 2

*Write **NO MORE THAN ONE WORD**, <u>or</u> circle the correct answer.*

1.   What is the subject of this morning's lecture?

....

2.   What time does the lecture begin?

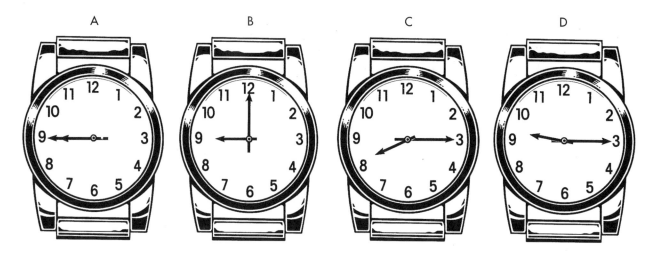

A   B   C   D

Question 3

Listen to the directions and find the Bradley Building. Choose the appropriate letter.

3.   Where is the Bradley Building?

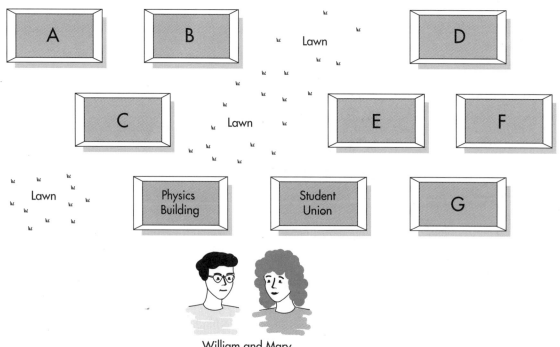

William and Mary

Questions 4–6

Circle the appropriate letter, A, B, C or D, as you listen.

4.   Which floor is Lecture Theatre H on?

A	fourth	**C**	eighth
B	sixth	**D**	tenth

5.   How do William and Mary go to Lecture Theatre H?

A	escalator, then lift	**C**	stairs only
B	lift, then stairs	**D**	stairs, then lift

6.   What does the sign say?

A

Lecture postponed until 10.00 today

C

Dr Jones ill — lecture cancelled today

B

Lecturer change — Professor Smith to present today's lecture

D

Lecture to be held in Theatre C today

Questions 7–11

Complete the table below.

Mary's timetable		
Class	**Day of week**	**Time**
Chemistry lecture	*Example* Tuesday	*Example* 10 o'clock
Chemistry lab	Wednesday	**(7)** .... o'clock
Genetics lecture	**(8)**	5 o'clock
Microbiology lecture	**(9)**	2 o'clock
Microbiology tutorial	Wednesday	**(10)** .... o'clock
Plant pathology lecture	Friday	**(11)** .... o'clock
Plant pathology lab	Tuesday	3 o'clock
Plant pathology tutorial	Wednesday	12 o'clock

Section 2   Questions 12–23

Questions 12–15

Complete the notes below. Write a **NUMBER** or **ONE WORD** for each answer.

The island of Astoria

12. • Distance from New Zealand: .... km

13. • Direction from New Zealand: ....

• Size compared with New Zealand: *Example*   25 per cent larger

14. • Shape of island: ....

15. • Climate: ....

Questions 16–23

Complete the table. Write a **NUMBER** or **NO MORE THAN TWO WORDS** for each answer.

The provinces of Astoria

Province	Part of island	Population	Language	Main tourist attraction
Hornchurch	**(16)**	*Example* 2.5 million	*Example* English	*Example* culture
New Devon	*Example* northeast	**(17)**	English	**(18)** . . . . . .
Anglezark		**(19)**	English	**(20)** . . . . . .
New Albion	**(21)**	1.5 million	**(22)**	**(23)** . . . . . .

Section 3 Questions 24–33

Questions 24–26

*Complete the table by ranking the **THREE** senses indicated.*

How did Immanuel Kant rank the senses?

	Sense	Ranking	
	touch		
24.	hearing	....	
25.	sight	....	
	smell	... 5 ...	*Example*
26.	taste	....	

Questions 27–29

Circle the correct answer.

27.   Immanuel Kant believed ...

	A	only smell was subjective.	C	touch was subjective.
	B	hearing was subjective.	D	smell was not necessary.

28.   A person who is 'odour-blind' ...

	A	can smell only some odours.	C	does not think flowers smell wonderful.
	B	is unable to smell flowers.	D	is probably colour-blind, too.

29.   The sense of smell ...

	A	is half as strong after the age of 65.	C	is stronger in women than men.
	B	is not affected by age.	D	is weakened in half of people over 80.

Questions 30–33

*Complete the sentences below. Write **NO MORE THAN TWO WORDS** for each answer.*

30.   The country that buys the most perfume is ....

31.   A perfume thought to be .... will sell well.

32.   French scientists believe the .... determines how a perfume will smell on a person.

33.   Some people who dislike perfume compare it to ....

Section 4   Questions 34–42

Questions 34 and 35

*Write **NO MORE THAN TWO WORDS** for each answer.*

34.   In Australia, when MUST men shake hands?   ....

35.   What is the message when men DON'T shake hands?   ....

Questions 36–42

*Match the gestures with their messages. Choose the appropriate letters **A–I** from the table. You may use a letter more than once.*

What message is sent by each of the following gestures?

FOR AUSTRALIAN MEN

Example	a weak handshake	D

36.   crushing handshake   ....

37.   half handshake   ....

38.   quickly released handshake   ....

39.   long handshake   ....

FOR AUSTRALIAN WOMEN

40.   half handshake   ....

41.   full, firm handshake   ....

FOR BOTH SEXES

42.   no eye contact during   ....
         handshake

A	no message
B	confidence
C	lack of confidence
D	lack of interest
E	arrogance
F	competence
G	competitiveness
H	mutual liking
I	recognition

IELTS Practice Listening Subtest

PAPER THREE

LENGTH OF TIME: 30 minutes
NUMBER OF QUESTIONS: 43

Audio Cassette Two, Side B

Instructions

- *This is a test to see how well you understand spoken English.*

- *You will hear several different recordings and you will have to answer questions on what you hear.*

- *The test is divided into four sections.*

- *There will be time for you to read the instructions and questions, and you will have a chance to check your work.*

- *You will hear each recording once only.*

- *(At the end of the real IELTS test, you will have ten minutes to transfer your answers to an answer sheet.)*

- *Now turn to Section 1 on the next page.*

Section 1   *Questions 1–11*

Questions 1–4

Circle the correct answer.

1.   What is Vincent's friend studying?

                A   biology   **C**   life sciences

                B   biochemistry   **D**   sociology

2.   What is the problem with the campus?

                A   distance from town   **C**   the food is bad

                B   strict student rules   **D**   few places to eat

3.   Sareena doesn't like the Union cafeteria because of . . .

                A   the lunchtime menu.   **C**   the music played there.

                B   the price of the food.   **D**   the quality of the food.

4.   Sareena doesn't want to go to the Aztec Grill because . . .

                A   she doesn't like Mexican **C**   the food is too spicy.
                          food.

                B   she prefers spicy food.   **D**   she doesn't like spicy food.

Question 5

*Circle the letter **A–E** for the appropriate building.*

5.   Where is the Luxor Cafe?

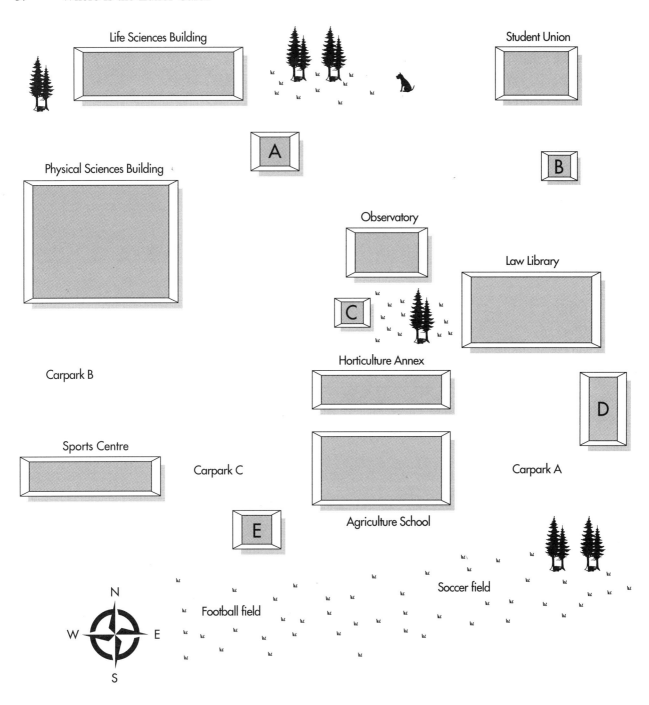

Questions 6–9

Tick (✓) the items that Sareena and Vincent order for lunch.

6.   What salads do Sareena and Vincent order?

Salad	Sareena	Vincent
Green salad	....	....
Greek salad	....	....
Seafood salad	....	*Example ... ✓ ...*
Caesar salad	....	....

7–9.   What else do Sareena and Vincent order? (*tick **THREE ITEMS** in total*)

Sandwich	Sareena	Vincent
Chicken	....	....
Roast beef	....	....
Horse	....	....
Tomato	....	....

Soup	Sareena	Vincent
Chicken	....	....
Onion	....	....
Tomato	....	....
Lemon	....	....

Questions 10 and 11

Circle the correct answer.

10.   On which day will Sareena and Vincent meet next week?

       A   Monday

       B   Tuesday

       C   Wednesday

       D   Thursday

       E   Friday

11.   What time do they agree to meet?

       A   12.15

       B   12.30

       C   12.45

       D   1.00

       E   1.15

Section 2   Questions 12–22

Questions 12–15

Write **NO MORE THAN TWO WORDS** or **NUMBERS** for each answer.

12.   On what basis does Alf Meerschaum divide Chapmanville into 3 areas?

....

13.   How much are the cheapest flats in eastern Chapmanville?

$............................ per month

14.   What is the price per month for a flat in the west or the south?

$............................ – $............................ per month

15.   Where is the cheapest accommodation?

Questions 16–22

*Complete the table. Write **NO MORE THAN TWO WORDS** for each answer.*

Region	Natural features	Disadvantages	Public transport
Northern Chapmanville	*Example* wetlands	(18)	buses
Southern Chapmanville	(16)	*Example* factories	(21) ......
Eastern Chapmanville	hills, trees		(22) ......
Western Chapmanville	(17)	(19) ...... (20)	*Example* trains, buses

Section 3   Questions 23–32

*Complete the notes from the lecture. Write **NO MORE THAN ONE NUMBER** or **TWO WORDS** for each answer.*

Example   • Most efficient material to recycle: *glass*

23.   — no loss of ....

24.   • Some bottle manufacturers in Japan, the US use 100% ....

25.   • Most bottle makers use about ....% recycled glass.

26.   • In the UK, ... are reused, not recycled.

27.   • Reusable bottles are recycled after being used .... times.

         • Obstacles to bottle reuse programs:

28.   — lack of ....

29.   — .... don't want to participate.

30.   • Consumers in Denmark and Canada must .... their bottles.

31.   • Making new plastic uses .... times more energy than recycling plastic.

32.   • Last environmental factor regarding bottles: ....

Section 4   Questions 33–43

Questions 33–36

*Circle **FOUR** letters.*

Identify FOUR sources of stress Fiona mentions.

    A   note-taking

    B   sitting examinations

    C   speaking to large groups

    D   getting to lectures on time

    E   anticipating assessment results

    F   writing essays

    G   speaking to lecturers

    H   assignment deadlines

    I   project planning

Questions 37 to 39

Tick (✓) the relevant boxes in each column.

How does the speaker rate the following events?

Event	(Question 37) Moderately stressful	(Question 38) Highly stressful	(Question 39) Extremely stressful
marriage		✓ *Example*	
divorce			
pregnancy			
school graduation			
spouse leaves work			

Question 40

Circle the best answer.

40.   Which is the most stressful event?

         A   shifting house

         B   retirement

         C   getting sacked from work

         D   conflict with spouse's mother

         E   holiday

Questions 41–43

*Complete the sentences below. Write **NO MORE THAN TWO WORDS** for each answer.*

41.   One sign of stress is .... with family members.

42.   Another sign of stress is .... despite a good diet.

43.   Another stress indicator is having trouble ....

Practice Reading *Papers*

The six Practice Reading Papers that follow should be attempted under test conditions. No dictionary or other reference book may be used and time limits must be strictly kept.

A photocopyable answer sheet is provided on page 65.

You may check your answers on pages 145–7.

IELTS to Success

Practice Reading Subtest
Answer sheet

1		22	
2		23	
3		24	
4		25	
5		26	
6		27	
7		28	
8		29	
9		30	
10		31	
11		32	
12		33	
13		34	
14		35	
15		36	
16		37	
17		38	
18		39	
19		40	
20		41	
21		42	

Practice IELTS Reading Subtest

Academic Module

PAPER ONE

TIME ALLOWED: 1 hour
NUMBER OF QUESTIONS: 42

Instructions

WRITE ALL YOUR ANSWERS ON THE ANSWER SHEET

The test is in 3 sections:

– –	Reading Passage 1	Questions 1–14
– –	Reading Passage 2	Questions 15–28
– –	Reading Passage 3	Questions 29–42

Remember to answer all the questions. If you are having trouble with a question, skip it and return to it later.

*You are advised to spend about 20 minutes on **Questions 1–14**, which are based on Reading Passage 1.*

Early Telecommunications Devices

Although it is hardly used anymore, the telegraph is familiar to most people. This early tele-communications device is credited, as any school student knows, to Samuel Morse, who, in 1844, made the first long-distance electronic communication via his invention, the Morse telegraph. What is not so commonly known is that Morse's was not the only telegraph nor he the only such inventor at this time. A rival system, developed by William Cooke and Charles Wheatstone, was patented in England in 1845 and was subsequently adopted for use by British rail companies to enable speedy communication between rail stations.

However, the Cooke–Wheatstone telegraph, which used six wires and a fragile receiver requiring five magnetic needles, proved to be awkward to use, difficult to transport and expensive to build. Morse's version used one wire and a receiver of a simpler and stronger design. This is, no doubt, why it became the favoured telegraph in many parts of the world, especially the United States, which built a telegraph line along railway tracks crossing the North American continent, linking eastern cities with western frontiers.

Morse chose the Magnetic Telegraph Company to handle the patents for his telegraph technology, and within seven years of the appearance of his invention, the company had licensed use of the tele-graph to more than 50 companies across the US. In 1851, twelve of these companies came together to form the Western Union Company. By 1866, Western Union had grown to include more than 4000 telegraph offices, almost all in rail stations.

Another early telecommunications device is still very much with us: the telephone. Although the telephone is popularly thought to be the brainchild of one man, Alexander Graham Bell, this is not the whole truth. Phillip Reis, a schoolteacher in Germany, invented a device in 1861 that he labelled a telephone. Reis's invention was limited to transmitting musical tones, however, and could not send the sound of the human voice across the wire.

While Reis was working on his invention, Bell and another man, Elisha Gray, were also working toward the invention of the telephone, though by an indirect route. Both were, in fact, seeking ways of allowing multiple telegraph signals to travel along the same telegraph line — a system known as a harmonic telegraph. Bell worked in Boston while Gray was based in Chicago, and the two were rivals in their area of research. For both inventors, the perfection of the harmonic telegraph proved too difficult and both, separately but at around the same time, changed plans and started on the development of a telephone. Most interesting of all is the fact that both men applied for a patent to the US Patent Office for their respective telephones on the same day, 14 February 1876. Bell was lucky enough to have arrived a few hours earlier than Gray and so it was Bell whose name was to be forever associated with the telephone. The harmonic telegraph, incidentally, was perfected by Thomas Edison, best known as the inventor of the light bulb, in 1881.

Rights to Bell's patent (now recognised as the most valuable patent in the history of technology) were offered to Western Union for $100 000, with the assumption that the giant telegraph company would be enthusiastic about the new technology. But Western Union disliked Bell's design and instead asked Elisha Gray to make refinements to his original telephone design. Bell's company began to set up its own business and sell telephones, while Western Union, with its somewhat different design, was its competitor.

(continued)

Competition between the two continued for about two years, but all the while, the Bell company was mounting a legal challenge to Western Union, claiming it held the only true basic patents for the telephone. It based its claim on the fact that Bell had beaten Gray to the Patent Office and so should be the sole recognised inventor of the telephone. Eventually, Western Union had to agree with Bell and gave up its telephone rights and patents to the Bell company. The telegraph company's entire network of telephones was handed over to the Bell company. As compensation, Western Union was given 20 per cent of revenue from rental of its former equipment; this arrangement was to last until Bell's patents expired. In an effort to fight the power the Bell company enjoyed from exclusive rights to Bell's patents, a small telephone company, Pacific Union, established telephone services in the 1920s and 1930s that it claimed were based on the telephone design of Phillip Reis. They maintained that because Reis's invention pre-dated Bell's, the Bell design was not the first of its kind and, therefore, Bell's patents were not valid. Although the court accepted that the company may have been using Reis's technology, it nonetheless held that only Bell's patents could legally be used.

The Bell company, eventually named American Telephone & Telegraph, thus formed an effective monopoly on telephone services in the United States. The company subsequently grew to such an extent that, a century later, it was the largest privately held enterprise in the world, with more than a million employees controlling communications between more than 100 million telephones. In 1984, American Telephone & Telegraph was found by a US court to be too monopolistic and was ordered to be broken up into several smaller companies.

---

patent: an official recognition of a person as the inventor of a device
monopoly: exclusive control of a market

Questions 1–5

*Complete the table below. Choose **NO MORE THAN THREE WORDS** from the passage for each answer. Write your answers in boxes 1–5 on your answer sheet.*

Year	Event	Inventor(s) (by surname)
1845	patent of telegraph	... (1) ...
1851	establishment of ... (2) ...	
1861	invention of telephone	... (3) ...
1876	application for patent of ... (4) ...	Gray
1881	successful development of ... (5) ...	Edison

Questions 6–10

Look at the following lists of inventors and companies. Match each inventor to **ONE** of the companies that used his/their technology. Choose *E* if there is no information in the reading passage. Write the appropriate letters **A–E** in boxes 6–10 on your answer sheet.

N.B.: You may use any letter more than once.

Inventors		Companies
Morse *Example**		**A** British rail companies
(6) Bell		**B** Pacific Union
(7) Cooke and Wheatstone		**C** American Telephone & Telegraph
(8) Edison		**D** Western Union
(9) Gray		*or*
(10) Reis		**E** no information in reading passage

*Example answer: D

Questions 11–14

USING NO MORE THAN THREE WORDS, answer the following questions. Write your answers in boxes 11–14 on your answer sheet.

11. Name ONE reason why Cooke and Wheatstone's invention was not as successful as Morse's.

12. In what type of location did Western Union typically offer its telegraph services?

13. What sort of information was Reis's original invention able to send?

14. What device did Alexander Graham Bell try but fail to invent?

*You are advised to spend about 20 minutes on **Questions 15–28**, which are based on Reading Passage 2.*

Categorising Love

Although many people would no doubt think it impossible, social psychologists over the past several decades have been attempting to categorise and quantify the notion of love. And while there may never be agreement on how this is best done, much of the research to date is quite thought-provoking.

Sternberg (1986) sees love in terms of the interplay between three independently quantifiable aspects: passion, intimacy and decision/commitment. Sternberg defines *passion* as the romantic and sexual components of a relationship. *Intimacy* is the degree of closeness a person feels for another. *Decision/commitment* concerns both one's decision about being in love with a person and, once in an established relationship with that person, how committed one is to loving one's partner.

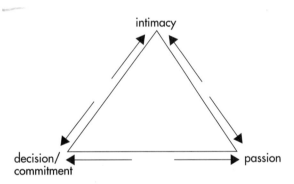

The intensity of each of the three aspects tells us how a love relationship can be characterised. If decision/commitment is strong, for example, but intimacy and passion are low, then the result is *empty love*, according to Sternberg. He defines *liking*, meanwhile, as the type of love resulting from a high degree of intimacy but low decision/commitment and passion. When passion is the only component that is strongly felt, this means that *infatuation* best describes the relationship. *Romantic love* occurs when there is a balance of passion and intimacy at relatively high levels but there is little decision/commitment. When all three aspects are more or less equally balanced, however, the relationship can be called one of *consummate love*,

and this, says Sternberg, is probably the healthiest in terms of the longevity of the relationship and the happiness of the partners.

In yet another categorisation of love, Lee (1973) divides the emotion into six different styles, each with its own name:

Love style	Characteristics
eros	romantic, passionate love; based on ideal images of one's partner
ludus	game-playing love; playful and teasing
storge	friendship love
pragma	practical, logical love; a 'shopping-list' approach to seeking a partner
mania	possessive, dependent love
agape	selfless, altruistic love; puts partner's interests above own

Lee believes most people feel or experience love as a combination of two or more of the above styles, and that both partners may approach their relationship with styles that are sometimes compatible and sometimes not. Hendrick and Hendrick (1986) investigated how men and women categorise their feelings and experiences of love using scales developed to measure Lee's six styles. They found that women scored higher on storge, pragma and mania styles, while men scored higher on ludus.

In a subsequent study, Hendrick and Adler (1988) looked at how men's and women's scores for the six love types correlated with satisfaction in their love relationships. The findings were that a relationship was more likely to be satisfactory if eros and agape scores for both partners were high, while a high score of ludus was more common in relationships marked by dissatisfaction.

The question of why different types or styles of love exist may best be addressed by attachment theory. The theory is based on observations of infants developing attachments to adults — interpreted by Bowlby (1980) as a natural, evolutionary behaviour that promotes survival of the infant by staying close to adults when there is danger. Ainsworth et al. (1978) divide attachment behaviour into three types: secure, anxious-ambivalent and avoidant. A *secure* attachment style forms when the infant and the care-giving adult interact with consistent caring and regular physical contact, giving the infant confidence to explore the world with little fear. When the adult gives care inconsistently or tries to interfere too much in the infant's activities, the attachment style is more likely to be *anxious-ambivalent*. An *avoidant* style results from regular refusal by the care-giving adult to give attention or physical contact to the infant.

Hazan and Shaver (1987), believing love to be a form of attachment, speculate that early attachment styles extend into adulthood and characterise a person's style of showing love for another person. They base their suppositions on the reported histories of over 1200 people, who wrote of both their adult romantic experience and their relationships with their parents. Adults with secure attachment styles reported that they found it fairly easy to get close to other people and enjoy a relationship characterised by mutual dependence. Moreover, there was little fear of being rejected by others. Those with avoidant attachment styles said they were not comfortable getting close to others, found it difficult to trust others completely and did not like having to rely on others. People in the anxious-ambivalent category felt their partners did not wish to become as intimate with them as they themselves would have liked. They also worried that they were not loved by their partners and constantly fretted about their romantic relationships.

Questions 15–19

On page 72 there are several diagrams illustrating the triangular relationship of passion, intimacy and decision/commitment, as defined by Sternberg (1986) in Reading Passage 2. Look at each diagram and determine whether it illustrates:

A   consummate love

B   romantic love

C   empty love

D   infatuation

E   liking

or

F   no information in the reading passage.

*Write the appropriate letters **A–F** in boxes 15–19 on your answer sheet.*

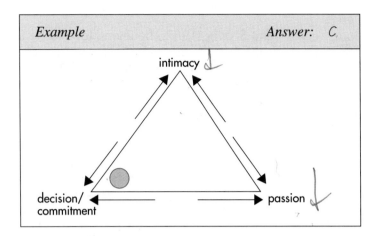

Example   Answer: C

intimacy

decision/
commitment   passion

15.

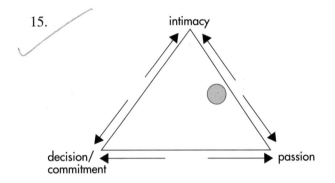

intimacy

decision/
commitment   passion

18.

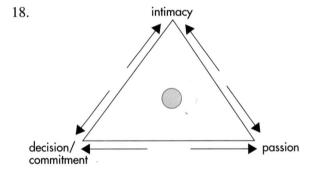

intimacy

decision/
commitment   passion

16.

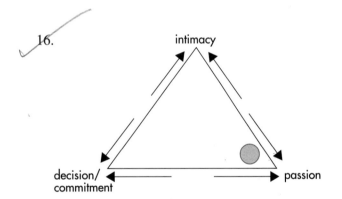

intimacy

decision/
commitment   passion

19.

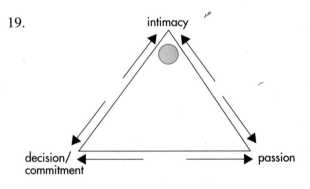

intimacy

decision/
commitment   passion

17.

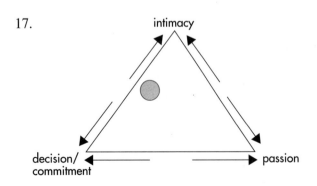

intimacy

decision/
commitment   passion

Questions 20–25

In Reading Passage 2, Lee (1973) divides love into six distinct styles. Each of the comments below can be attributed to a person with one of those styles. Classify the comments as typical of:

      A   agape

      B   eros

      C   ludus

      D   mania

      E   pragma

      F   storge

*Write the appropriate letters **A–F** in boxes 20–25 on your answer sheet.*

Example

    'I would rather suffer myself than let my partner suffer.'

Answer: A

---

20.   'Our relationship is satisfying because it developed from a deep friendship.'

21.   'I can't relax if I suspect my partner is with somebody else. I want him/her all to myself.'

22.   'When I chose my partner, I considered how he/she would affect my career ambitions.'

23.   'My partner looks just like the kind of person I've always wanted to be with. I was attracted to him/her as soon as we met.'

24.   'I wouldn't hesitate to give everything I own to my partner if he/she wanted it.'

25.   'I like to keep my partner guessing whether I really love him/her.'

Questions 26–28

*Complete the sentences below with words taken from Reading Passage 2. Use **NO MORE THAN TWO WORDS** for each answer. Write your answers in boxes 26–28 on your answer sheet.*

26.   If adults consistently withdraw from contact with an infant, the likely result will be a(n) _____ attachment style.

27.   Adults with _____ attachment styles tend to wish for more closeness from their partners than they are getting.

28.   Dependence on others may present a problem for people with _____ attachment styles.

READING PASSAGE 3

*You should spend about 20 minutes on **Questions 29–42**, which are based on Reading Passage 3.*

Questions 29–33

Reading Passage 3 has 6 paragraphs.

*Choose the most suitable headings for paragraphs **B–F** from the list of headings below. Write the appropriate numbers (**i–ix**) in boxes 29–33 on your answer sheet.*

N.B.: There are more headings than paragraphs so you will not use all of them. You may use any of the headings more than once.

List of headings

(i) Responsibilities of responding police officers

(ii) Perceived advantages of rapid response

(iii) Police response to public satisfaction

(iv) Communicating response time to people requesting help

(v) When rapid response is and is not necessary

(vi) Role of technology in improving police response

(vii) Response time and success of response

(viii) Public demand for catching criminals

(ix) Obstacles to quickly contacting the police

Example	
Paragraph A	*Answer:* vi

29. Paragraph B

30. Paragraph C

31. Paragraph D

32. Paragraph E

33. Paragraph F

Rapid Police Response

A   Police departments in the United States and Canada see it as central to their role that they respond to calls for help as quickly as possible. This ability to react fast has been greatly improved with the aid of technology. The telephone and police radio, already long in use, assist greatly in the reduction of police response time. In more recent times there has been the introduction of the '911' emergency system, which allows the public easier and faster contact with police, and the use of police computer systems, which assist police in planning patrols and assigning emergency requests to the police officers nearest to the scene of the emergency.

B   An important part of police strategy, rapid police response is seen by police officers and the public alike as offering tremendous benefits. The more obvious ones are the ability of police to apply first-aid life-saving techniques quickly and the greater likelihood of arresting people who may have participated in a crime. It aids in identifying those who witnessed an emergency or crime, as well as in collecting evidence. The overall reputation of a police department, too, is enhanced if rapid response is consistent, and this in itself promotes the prevention of crime. Needless to say, rapid response offers the public some degree of satisfaction in its police force.

C   While these may be the desired consequences of rapid police response, actual research has not shown it to be quite so beneficial. For example, it has been demonstrated that rapid response leads to a greater likelihood of arrest only if responses are in the order of 1–2 minutes after a call is received by the police. When response times increase to 3–4 minutes — still quite a rapid response — the likelihood of an arrest is substantially reduced. Similarly, in identifying witnesses to emergencies or crimes, police are far more likely to be successful if they arrive at the scene no more than four minutes, on average, after receiving a call for help. Yet both police officers and the public define 'rapid response' as responding up to 10–12 minutes after calling the police for help.

D   Should police assume all the responsibility for ensuring a rapid response? Studies have shown that people tend to delay after an incident occurs before contacting the police. A crime victim may be injured and thus unable to call for help, for example, or no telephone may be available at the scene of the incident. Often, however, there is no such physical barrier to calling the police. Indeed, it is very common for crime victims to call their parents, their minister, or even their insurance company first. When the police are finally called in such cases, the effectiveness of even the most rapid of responses is greatly diminished.

(continued)

E   The effectiveness of rapid response also needs to be seen in light of the nature of the crime. For example, when someone rings the police after discovering their television set has been stolen from their home, there is little point, in terms of identifying those responsible for the crime, in ensuring a very rapid response. It is common in such burglary or theft cases that the victim discovers the crime hours, days, even weeks after it has occurred. When the victim is directly involved in the crime, however, as in the case of a robbery, rapid response, provided the victim was quickly able to contact the police, is more likely to be advantageous. Based on statistics comparing crimes that are discovered and those in which the victim is directly involved, Spelman and Brown (1981) suggest that three in four calls to police need not be met with rapid response.

F   It becomes clear that the importance of response time in collecting evidence or catching criminals after a crime must be weighed against a variety of factors. Yet because police department officials assume the public strongly demands rapid response, they believe that every call to the police should be met with it. Studies have shown, however, that while the public wants quick response, more important is the information given by the police to the person asking for help. If a caller is told the police will arrive in five minutes but in fact it takes ten minutes or more, waiting the extra time can be extremely frustrating. But if a caller is told he or she will have to wait 10 minutes and the police indeed arrive within that time, the caller is normally satisfied. Thus, rather than emphasising rapid response, the focus of energies should be on establishing realistic expectations in the caller and making every effort to meet them.

Questions 34 and 35

Name the **TWO LATEST** *technological developments that reduce police response time. Using* **NO MORE THAN THREE WORDS** *for each answer, write the two developments separately in boxes 34–35 on your answer sheet.*

Questions 36–42

Do the following statements reflect the claims of the writer in Reading Passage 3? In boxes 36–42 write:

YES	*if the statement reflects the writer's claims*
NO	*if the statement contradicts the writer*
NOT GIVEN	*if there is no information about this in the passage*

36.   Police believe there is a better chance of finding witnesses to a crime if response is rapid.

37.   A response delay of 1–2 minutes may have substantial influence on whether or not a suspected criminal is caught.

38.   The public and the police generally agree on the amount of time normally taken for a rapid response.

39.   Physical barriers are the greatest cause of delay in contacting police.

40.   Rapid response is considered desirable in handling cases of burglary.

41.   Research shows that some 75 per cent of crimes are discovered by victims after they have been committed.

42.   Police departments are usually successful in providing a rapid response regardless of the circumstances of the crime or emergency.

Practice IELTS Reading Subtest

Academic Module

PAPER TWO

TIME ALLOWED: 1 hour
NUMBER OF QUESTIONS: 37

Instructions

WRITE ALL YOUR ANSWERS ON THE ANSWER SHEET

The test is in 3 sections:

– –	Reading Passage 1	Questions 1–10
– –	Reading Passage 2	Questions 11–22
– –	Reading Passage 3	Questions 23–37

Remember to answer all the questions. If you are having trouble with a question, skip it and return to it later.

READING PASSAGE 1

*You should spend about 20 minutes on **Questions 1–10**, which are based on Reading Passage 1.*

High-school Students in Part-time Employment: What Effect on Scholastic Performance?

Educators in the United States have long argued about the effects of part-time work on the academic performance of high-school students. Though many studies claim that there is a relationship between a student's grade point average (GPA) — the standard measure of academic performance in high schools and universities in the US — and the number of hours the student is employed, there seems little agreement on what that relationship is.

Several studies (Sneider 1982; Wallace 1988; Johnson & Payne 1989) suggest that students who work after school do better in their school work than students who do not have a job. Peel and Maas (1990), meanwhile, suggest that students with part-time jobs generally do worse in school than their classmates who do not work at all. Still other research claims the number of hours worked outside school hours is of very minor importance; much more important in influencing a student's performance in school are the student's study habits and home life (Alvarez 1987).

Of seven major studies on high-school students in employment reviewed by Bjarnes and Doi (1990), four studies specifically investigated the relationship between scholastic achievement and part-time work. Of these, two concluded that students who work more than a certain number of hours per week tend to have generally lower GPAs (Walston & Yin 1990; Corbelli 1989). These two studies noted the positive correlation between the number of hours worked and improved academic achievement when work hours are no more than about 12 per week. However, when employment took up 20 hours or more of a student's week, a negative correlation became evident: GPAs decreased as job hours grew.

In a more recent investigation, Krunjic (1995) surveyed some 1000 students each in grades 10, 11 and 12. (Students in these grades were chosen because they are more likely to have jobs than students in other grades.) The students were from six high schools of different size in southern California. Two of the high schools were located in rural areas, two in large cities and two in suburban areas. Students were asked to fill out questionnaires about their GPA and the hours they worked.

Some of the results of Krunjic's survey are illustrated in the figures below. Krunjic found that beyond approximately 5 hours per week, the more hours a student worked, the lower his or her GPA (figure 1). This relationship between GPA and work appeared to be stronger the lower the grade level (figure 2). Comparing academic performance and geographic location, Krunjic found that the GPAs of both rural and urban students were less influenced by how many hours worked than were those of suburban students.

Krunjic also looked at differences between males and females. Equal numbers of high-school girls and boys were in jobs, but in jobs of fewer hours, girls outnumbered boys. As the number of hours at work increased, there was a greater number of boys and a smaller number of girls (figure 3).

Krunjic concluded from the survey data that while both his and some earlier studies showed that an increase in hours worked brings a decrease in GPA, the decrease is not serious enough to worry educators greatly. Krunjic goes on to suggest, however, that schools and boards of education become well acquainted with this relationship before deciding whether or by how much to limit the number of hours students can work.

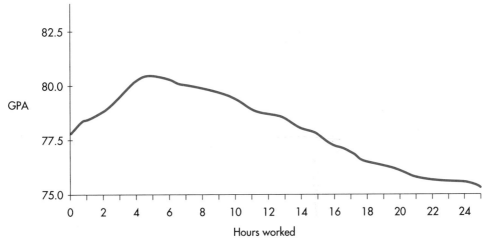

Figure 1: Average GPA and hours worked, all students

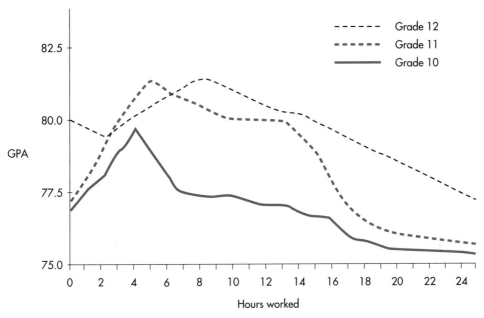

Figure 2: Average GPA and hours worked, by grade level

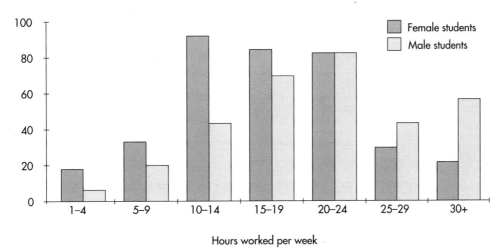

Figure 3: High-school girls and boys in employment

The paragraph below is a partial summary of Reading Passage 1. Complete the summary by choosing your answers from the list below and writing them in boxes 1–4 on your answer sheet.

N.B.: There are more choices than spaces so you will not use them all. You may use any of the choices more than once.

Research into the effects of part-time work on high-school students' academic performance has produced a variety of conclusions. According to … *(Example)* …, we can expect students with jobs to perform better in school than students not working at all. Indeed, … **(1)** … believe(s) that the more hours worked, the better the scholastic performance of the student, though this correlation drops off once a student works more than a dozen hours a week. … **(2)** … found much the same results but that the improvement in GPA dropped off with even fewer hours per week. But still other researchers, such as … **(3)** …, believe that no amount of employment hours, however few or many, improves academic performance. And according to … **(4)** …, factors other than working hours have a far greater influence on GPA.

Example answer: D

A	Alvarez (1987)
B	Bjarnes & Doi (1990)
C	Corbelli (1989)
D	Johnson & Payne (1989)
E	Krunjic (1995)
F	Peel & Maas (1990)

*Complete the sentences below with **NUMBERS** taken from Reading Passage 1. Write your answers in boxes 5–8 on your answer sheet.*

The following statements refer to the research of Krunjic (1995).

5. Overall, students in grade _____ were the least likely to suffer poor academic performance with increasing work hours.

6. Grade _____ students working 4–5 hours per week achieved a higher average GPA than students in other grades.

7. Girls were more likely than boys to work in jobs of up to _____ hours.

8. Boys were as likely as girls to work in jobs of _____ hours.

Question 9

*Complete the following sentence with **NO MORE THAN TWO WORDS** taken from Reading Passage 1. Write your answer in box 9 on your answer sheet.*

9.   According to Krunjic (1995), having a part-time job is most likely to affect students in high schools located in _____ .

Question 10

*Choose the appropriate letter **A–D** and write it in box 10 on your answer sheet.*

10.   Krunjic (1995) believes that school officials . . .

        A   need not take seriously the results of his research.

        B   worry about the relationship between GPA and part-time work.

        C   should limit the number of hours students can work.

        D   need to understand the relationship between GPA and part-time work.

READING PASSAGE 2

*You are advised to spend about 20 minutes on **Questions 11–22**, which are based on Reading Passage 2.*

Fish Oil

Much has been made of the benefits of oil derived from fish. It is claimed that people with a diet rich in fish oil have a greatly reduced chance of heart disease and arteriosclerosis. In addition, it has been shown conclusively that people suffering from elevated blood lipids react positively to treatment using fish oils.

The advantages of fish oil became apparent after studies some two decades ago of the diet of the Inuit, or Eskimo, populations of Greenland. It was found that the Inuit, with their traditional diet of seal, whale and Arctic fish — a diet very high in fat — suffered practically no heart disease, had near zero incidence of diabetes and enjoyed a comparatively low rate of rheumatoid arthritis. (Interestingly, incidence of cancer, equal to that found in most other parts of the world, appeared unaffected by the traditional Inuit diet.)

Until the work of Dyberg and Bang in the 1970s, little attention was paid to the implications of a fish-rich diet, despite a centuries-old knowledge of Inuit customs. The two researchers noted that in one community of 1800 people there were only three heart attack deaths between 1950 and 1974. To understand why, they examined the Inuits' blood lipids and diet. Omega-3 fatty acids featured strongly in the bloodstream of the research subjects, directly attributable to diet.

In order to rule out genetic or racial factors from their findings, Dyberg and Bang went on to compare the Greenland Inuit communities with those Inuit residing in Denmark who consumed a diet almost identical to that of the Danes. The Inuit in Denmark, particularly those who had been there for longer

(continued)

periods, were shown to have higher blood cholesterol levels and significantly higher serum triglyceride levels than their Greenland counterparts. In fact, the levels of the Westernised Inuits matched those of the Danes themselves, who consume mainly meat, milk products and eggs. As would be expected, levels of heart disease and arteriosclerosis of the Inuit well-established in Denmark were far closer to those of the Danes than those of the Greenland Inuit. The findings, according to the researchers, indicated an Omega-3 deficiency in the Danish diet compared with the Greenland diet.

Similar findings come from Japan. A comparison of the diets of farmers and fishermen, together with an examination of health records and death rates of the two groups, has shown a link between the health of the human heart and fish oil. Whereas the average Japanese farmer has 90 grams of fish a day, the average fisherman has 250 grams. In all other respects, their diets are similar. Correspondingly, fishermen have lower blood pressure and lower rates of heart disease and rheumatoid arthritis. This compares with the 20 grams eaten daily by the average person in the US, where rates of heart disease and arteriosclerosis are five to seven times higher than in Japan.

Its high Omega-3 content and easy digestibility make fish oil particularly useful in the treatment of hyperlipidaemic patients. Studies have shown an inverse relationship between dosage of salmon oil and plasma triglyceride concentrations. Specifically, it has been found that the consumption of three grams of salmon oil per day by such patients reduces their plasma triglyceride levels some 32 per cent. For patients given six grams, the levels fall by 41 per cent, and for those taking nine grams, concentrations dropped an average of 52 per cent.

Table 1, below, gives the Omega-3 contents of several fish varieties as compared with a selection of vegetable-based oils and butterfat.

Table 1: Omega-3 fatty acid content of selected fish and vegetable oils and butterfat

Oil source	Proportion Omega-3 fatty acids in oil (%)
Salmon	60
Mackerel	62
Tuna	58
Anchovy	71
Linseed	49
Soybean	7
Olive	1
Peanut	0
Butterfat	2.5

Questions 11–15

*Using the information in Reading Passage 2, indicate the relationship between the two items given for each question **11–15** on page 83 by marking on your answer sheet:*

PC   if there is a positive correlation

NC   if there is a negative correlation

L/N   if there is little or no correlation

NI   if there is no information.

*Write your answers (**PC**, **NC**, **L/N**, or **NI**) in boxes 11–15 on your answer sheet.*

Example	proportion of traditional foods in diet	heart disease among Greenland Inuit	Answer: NC
11.	proportion of traditional foods in diet	incidence of cancer among Greenland Inuit	
12.	Inuits' length of stay in Denmark	serum triglyceride levels	
13.	amount of meat consumed	consumption of Omega-3 fatty acids	
14.	'Westernisation' of Inuit diet	consumption of Omega-3 fatty acids	
15.	daily salmon dosage	plasma triglyceride levels	

Questions 16–22

Do the following statements reflect the claims of the writer in Reading Passage 2? In boxes 16–22 on your answer sheet, write:

YES	*if the statement reflects the writer's claims*
NO	*if the statement contradicts the writer*
NOT GIVEN	*if there is no information about this in the passage.*

16. Diabetes is rare among the Greenland Inuit.

17. The Greenland Inuits' rheumatoid arthritis levels are the lowest in the world.

18. Little was known about Inuit life in Greenland before the work of Dyberg and Bang.

19. Blood cholesterol levels of the Denmark Inuit were lower than those of the Danes.

20. Research in Japan generally supports the findings of Dyberg and Bang with regard to the effects of fish oil.

21. Greenland Inuit and Japanese fishermen consume similar amounts of Omega-3 fatty acids.

22. Anchovy oil contains about ten times the proportion of Omega-3 fatty acids contained in an equal measure of soybean oil.

READING PASSAGE 3

*You should spend about 20 minutes on **Questions 23–37**, which are based on Reading Passage 3.*

Questions 23–28

Reading Passage 3 has 7 sections.

*Choose the most suitable headings for sections **B–G** from the list of headings below. Write the appropriate numbers (**i–x**) in boxes 23–28 on your answer sheet.*

N.B.: There are more headings than sections so you will not use all of them. You may use any of the headings more than once.

List of headings

(i) Benefits of bicycle use: one country's experience

(ii) Situations that best fit bicycle use

(iii) Factors working against NMV use

(iv) The disadvantages of cycle rickshaw use

(v) The continuing importance of NMVs in Asia

(vi) Subsidising public transport use in China

(vii) Appropriate use of cycle rickshaws

(viii) Use of NMVs to reduce motorisation in Europe

(ix) The role of policy in promoting bicycle use

(x) Integrated approach to urban transport

Example		
Section A	*Answer:*	v

23. Section B

24. Section C

25. Section D

26. Section E

27. Section F

28. Section G

Non-Motorised Vehicles in Asia

Section A

Non-motorised vehicles (NMVs), which include bicycles, cycle rickshaws and carts, continue to play a vital role in urban transport in much of Asia. NMVs account for 25 to 80 per cent of vehicle trips in many Asian cities, more than anywhere else in the world. Ownership of all vehicles, including NMVs, is growing rapidly throughout Asia as incomes increase.

Section B

However, the future of NMVs in many Asian cities is threatened by growing motorisation, loss of street space for safe NMV use, and changes in urban form prompted by motorisation. Transport planning and investment in most of Asia has focused principally on the motorised transport sector and has often ignored the needs of non-motorised transport.

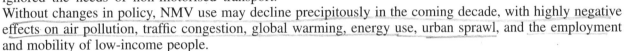

Cycle rickshaw

Without changes in policy, NMV use may decline precipitously in the coming decade, with highly negative effects on air pollution, traffic congestion, global warming, energy use, urban sprawl, and the employment and mobility of low-income people.

Section C

As cities in Japan, the Netherlands, Germany and several other European nations demonstrate, the modernisation of urban transport does not require total motorisation, but rather the appropriate integration of walking, NMV modes and motorised transport. As in European and Japanese cities, where a major share of trips are made by walking and cycling, NMVs have an important role to play in urban transport systems throughout Asia in coming decades.

Section D

Transport investment and policy are the primary factors that influence NMV use and can have an effect on the pace and level of motorisation. For example, Japan has witnessed major growth of bicycle use, despite increased motorisation, through programs providing extensive bicycle paths, bicycle parking at rail stations and high fees for motor vehicle use. Denmark and the Netherlands have reversed the decline of bicycle use through similar policies.

Section E

China has for several decades offered commuter subsidies for those people bicycling to work, cultivated a domestic bicycle manufacturing industry and allocated extensive urban street space to NMV traffic. This strategy reduced the growth of public transport subsidies while meeting most mobility needs. Bicycles have largely replaced buses as the principal means of urban vehicular transport in Tianjin. Buses are generally slower for the same trip made by bicycle. Today, 50 to 80 per cent of urban vehicle trips in China are by bicycle and average journey times in China's cities appear to be comparable to those of many other more motorised Asian cities, with much more favourable consequences on the environment, petroleum dependency, transport system costs and traffic safety.

Section F

Bicycles should be encouraged as the most efficient transport mode for short trips in cities of all types, particularly for trips too long for walking and too short for express public transport services or where travel demand or economics do not permit high-frequency public transport services. Bicycles are most important for personal transport, but also accommodate light goods, being capable of carrying loads of 100–180 kilograms.

(continued)

Section G

Cycle rickshaws are not as efficient as bicycles for personal transport, but should be encouraged as a complementary mode to motorised goods transport and as a passenger transit mode, particularly in countries where low wages and surplus labour are substantial features of the economy. Where they are in use, they should be accepted as a useful part of the transportation system rather than as a nuisance or a barrier to transport system modernisation. Even in high-income, motor-vehicle-dependent cities, there are opportunities for appropriate use of cycle rickshaws for short-distance movement of persons and goods and as the basis for small businesses providing goods and services at dispersed locations. They find greatest utility where slow modes of transport are allocated road space separate from motorised traffic, in neighbourhoods where the majority of people go from one place to another on foot or in central areas with slow traffic speeds, in large factories and shopping districts, and areas where private automobiles are restricted.

Questions 29–32

In Reading Passage 3, the author mentions several ways in which bicycle use in cities is encouraged.

From the list below, identify **FOUR** such ways. Write the appropriate letters **A–G** in boxes 29–32 on your answer sheet.

A	establishing routes especially for bicycles
B	removing buses from streets
C	restricting parts of road from motorised traffic
D	educating public about environmental effects of motor vehicle use
E	encouraging public transport users to bicycle to train stations
F	reducing bicycle manufacturing costs
G	making motor vehicle use more expensive

Questions 33–37

Complete the notes below. Use **NO MORE THAN TWO WORDS** from the passage for each answer. Write your answers in boxes 33–37 on your answer sheet.

CYCLE RICKSHAWS

- best in economies with ... **(33)** ... & ... **(34)** ...

- best for:
  — transporting people and goods short distances
  — helping ... **(35)** ... make widely separated deliveries

- best where:
  — motorised and non-motorised traffic are separate
  — most people travel ... **(36)** ...
  — traffic is kept slow
  — there are large factories
  — there are shopping centres
  — limited use of ... **(37)** ...

Practice IELTS Reading Subtest

Academic Module

PAPER THREE

TIME ALLOWED: 1 hour
NUMBER OF QUESTIONS: 41

Instructions

WRITE ALL YOUR ANSWERS ON THE ANSWER SHEET

The test is in 3 sections:

- – Reading Passage 1   Questions 1–13

- – Reading Passage 2   Questions 14–28

- – Reading Passage 3   Questions 29–41

Remember to answer all the questions. If you are having trouble with a question, skip it and return to it later.

*You are advised to spend about 15 minutes on **Questions 1–13**, which are based on Reading Passage 1.*

Building Houses out of Earth

On every continent, one can find houses or other buildings made of the clay-bearing soils dug up from the ground. In some places, earth building technologies have been around for a very long time. In the southwestern United States, for example, American Indian tribes such as the Pueblo people have been building earth houses and other earth structures for thousands of years. And in China's Xinjiang Province, archaeologists have found entire earth villages dating back over 2500 years. While building houses out of earth is certainly not new, it has never been very common because of the preference for other materials.

In some parts of the world, however, there has been renewed growth in the popularity of earth building. Two such places are Australia and New Zealand, where the practice did not exist until the relatively recent arrival of European settlers. It is estimated that there are now more than 2100 houses made of earth in Australia, and 35 per cent of them were built within the past decade. An equal proportion of the 550 earthen structures in New Zealand were built in the last five years. This trend appears to reflect growing earth construction in North America and Western Europe.

Why the renewed interest in earth building? The building material itself is probably the reason. Earth is available virtually anywhere, literally under our feet. And unlike many other building materials that typically require treatment with chemical preservatives, earth is non-toxic. This cannot be said for commercially sold timber and brick products.

Another well-known characteristic of earth houses is their passive solar capacity — their ability to retain warmth in the winter and keep cool in the summer without the need for dedicated solar panels, plumbing or fossil fuel energy sources. This comes entirely from the effective way in which the earthen walls act to store heat.

Some people claim that earth buildings are cheaper to build than conventional brick or wooden houses, the two most common types in Australia and New Zealand. This appears to be true, according to data from the *New Zealand Construction Quarterly*. Assuming walls make up 15 per cent of the cost of building a house, then the use of earthen walls would bring a total saving of 10 per cent over timber frame construction and 38 per cent over brick.

But perhaps most attractive of all is the unique atmosphere provided by earth houses, with their natural colours, their acoustic properties and thick, solid walls.

Not all earth building is done the same way. The technologies used vary from region to region, depending on the types of earth available and local building traditions. They are also undergoing constant study and improvement, with a view to bettering resistance to earthquakes and weather.

In New Zealand, stabilisers such as cement, sand, straw, even cow dung, have been found to make a stronger and longer-lasting material when added to earth. The downside of using particularly effective stabilisers like cement is that they can be expensive and their manufacture may create much pollution. Thus their use should be kept to a minimum.

Those who choose to build with earth should also be careful about using paints or other coatings on the surface of the earth walls. Some coatings have the effect of preventing the walls from 'breathing'. When this happens any water that gets absorbed into the walls may not have a way of escaping and so gets trapped. This may lead to cracks or other signs of early deterioration of the earthen material.

Question 1

Choose the appropriate letter (A–D) and write it in box 1 on your answer sheet.

1.   In 'Building houses out of earth', the writer's main aim is to . . .

                A   provide an overview of earth building.

                B   promote the building of earth houses.

                C   review the history of earth building.

                D   examine the variety of earth buildings.

Questions 2 and 3

2.   Name **TWO** places where earth building practices have existed for a long time.

Write the names of the places in box 2 on your answer sheet.

3.   Name **THREE** places where earth building is becoming more popular.

Write the names of the places in box 3 on your answer sheet.

Questions 4–7

In 'Building houses out of earth', the writer mentions several reasons why some people prefer earth houses. Read the list of reasons below and choose **FOUR** that are referred to in the passage.

Write your answers in boxes 4–7 on your answer sheet.

                A   cost of construction

                B   resistance to earthquakes

                C   stability of earth

                D   heat storage capacity

                E   availability of materials

                F   construction technology

                G   appearance and character

Questions 8–11

*Using a **NUMBER** or **NO MORE THAN THREE WORDS**, answer the following questions. Write your answers in boxes 8–11 on your answer sheet.*

8. What percentage of earth buildings in New Zealand were constructed in the past 5 years?

9. Name **ONE** building material that contains chemical preservatives.

10. Name the feature of earth houses that enables them to keep temperatures low in summer.

11. Name **TWO** substances that can lengthen the life of earth as a building material.

Questions 12 and 13

*Complete the flow chart below. Choose **ONE** or **TWO** words from the passage for each answer.*

Write your answers in boxes 12–13 on your answer sheet.

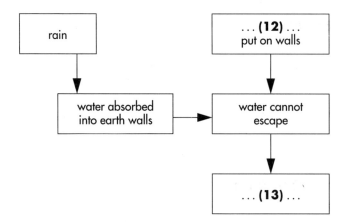

READING PASSAGE 2

*You should spend about 25 minutes on **Questions 14–28**, which are based on Reading Passage 2.*

Book-Carrying Behaviour

Psychologists have long observed that women and men perform certain physical actions in different ways. One such action is the carrying of books. Howard and White (1966) maintain that there is a 'masculine' style and a 'feminine' style of book carrying and that one's sex determines which of these styles one will use.

In observations of over 3600 university students in North and South America, Howard and White recorded five styles of book carrying. These styles, labelled 'A', 'B', 'C', 'D' and 'E', were then categorised into two main types: Type I and Type II. Howard and White's categorisations are given in detail in the box on the next page.

Type I

A. The books cover part of the front of the body. The books' short edges are parallel to the ground and rest against the body. One arm is wrapped around the books, with the elbow bent and the fingers wrapped around the books' long edges.

B. The same as A above, except both arms are wrapped around the books, which are usually more centred in front of the body.

Type II

C. The books are held at the side of the body and so do not cover any part of the front. The arms are kept straight and the books are held, in one hand, from above. The books' long edges are parallel to the ground.

D. As C above, but the books are held from below, with the fingers wrapped around the lower edges.

E. As D above, except the elbows are bent and the books are raised along the side of the body.

Other

Positions characteristic of neither Type I nor Type II.

Howard and White's findings were that men and women differ markedly in the way they carry books. They reported that some 82 per cent of females use Type I methods while 16 per cent use Type II. For men, Type II methods were used by 96 per cent whereas only 3 per cent used the 'feminine' style.

A smaller study in the UK by Haldern and Matthews (1969) confirmed the distinction in book-carrying styles, and went on to explain this difference in terms of male and female body shape and strength. The researchers claimed morpho-anatomical features, such as hip and shoulder width, as well as the strength of the fingers and hands, were the main determinants of carrying styles for males and females.

Subsequent research into the relationship of age to carrying behaviour (Namimitsu & Matthews 1971) found that there was little or no difference between the sexes among kindergarten children, and that a large majority of children of either sex carried books in the manner of Type II. Wilson (1972) found that by primary school, differences began to emerge along the lines of Howard and White's 'feminine' and 'masculine' styles — that is, girls' carrying positions began to diverge from boys'. Children in the 14–16 age group were found to display the greatest difference in book-carrying behaviour, with some 91 per cent of girls using Type I methods (Agfitz 1972a). In his review of the research done up to that time, Wilson (1976) stressed that in all the studies into developmental aspects of the behaviour, male carrying behaviour remained broadly consistent throughout the age groups, including the university students who were the subjects of Howard and White's (1966) study. Studies of older adult age groups showed a decreasing, yet enduring, gap in styles as people aged. With increasing age, increasing numbers of women were shown to abandon Type I in favour of Type II (Agfitz 1972b).

Looking at other possible explanations for these differences, Agfitz (1973) offered the notion of social pressure on children to conform to behaviours 'typical' of their sex. This is especially the case in the context of secondary school, where children are pressured by their fellow students to conform to behaviours that society considers normal.

In the early 1990s, this notion of book-carrying behaviour as gender-specific came under review. Vilberberg and Zhou (1991), in making the first large-scale observational study since Howard and White (1966), found that women of university age and older were as likely to use Type II methods as Type I. Observing some 3750 university students and adult public-library users in Holland and

(continued)

Belgium, the researchers found that while 92 per cent of males exhibited Type II behaviour, only 52 per cent of females used Type I methods. Some 47 per cent carried books in the manner of Type II. Most interestingly, of this latter proportion, more than three-quarters used style 'E'.

The notion of 'feminine' and 'masculine' book-carrying styles was suddenly thrown into doubt, as Chadamitsky (1993) and others argued that carrying behaviour could not be claimed to be gender-specific if females were not consistent in the styles they displayed. Male carrying behaviour, even in the Vilberberg and Zhou study, remained a virtual constant, and so could be labelled 'typical' for males. But because this style was well shared by females, it could not be called 'masculine'. Chadamitsky went on to argue that the original interpretation of Howard and White's (1966) study — that there were clear 'feminine' and 'masculine' styles — set the course of subsequent research in that direction. Future research, he argued, should look not at why females and males display different book-carrying behaviours, but why males are uniform and females are more apt to vary.

---

gender-specific: particular to either males or females

Questions 14–17

Classify the following book-carrying styles as:

       A   Style 'A'

       B   Style 'B'

       C   Style 'C'

       D   Style 'D'

       E   Style 'E'

OR

       O   Other.

*Write the appropriate letters **A–O** in boxes 14–17 on your answer sheet.*

14.  15.  16.  17.

Questions 18–24

*Below is a list of research conclusions mentioned in Reading Passage 2. Indicate which researcher(s) was/were responsible for each research conclusion by writing their **NAMES AND PUBLICATION YEARS** in boxes 18–24 on your answer sheet.*

Research conclusions

> *Example*
>
> Types I and II can reasonably be labelled 'feminine' and 'masculine' behaviours, respectively.
>
> *Answer:* Howard and White (1966)

18. The influence on children to fit into socially accepted roles may contribute to differences in carrying behaviour.

19. Young teenage girls were most likely to use Type I methods.

20. 'Feminine' and 'masculine' carrying styles may be accounted for by anatomical differences in female and male bodies.

21. There is no consistent male–female difference in book-carrying behaviour in early childhood.

22. Males of all ages appear to be consistent in their carrying behaviour.

23. Close to half of women carry in such a way that books cover no part of the front of their body.

24. Older women are less likely than younger women to display Type I methods.

Questions 25–28

Do the following statements reflect the claims of the writer in Reading Passage 2? In boxes 25–28 write:

YES	*if the statement reflects the writer's claims*
NO	*if the statement contradicts the writer*
NOT GIVEN	*if there is no information about this in the passage.*

25. Researchers in the 1990s suggested the notion that social, rather than physical, factors better explain differences in book-carrying style.

26. In the Vilberberg and Zhou (1991) study, the majority of women using Type II methods used style 'E'.

27. Vilberberg and Zhou's (1991) findings weaken Howard and White's (1966) conclusions about gender-specific book-carrying behaviour.

28. Chadamitsky (1993) suggested that, in the future, research ought to be directed at why both male and female book-carrying behaviours vary.

*You are advised to spend about 20 minutes on **Questions 29–41**, which are based on Reading Passage 3.*

Television News

Critics of television news often complain that news programs do not make enough of an effort to inform the viewer, that the explanations they give of events are too short, too simple, lacking depth, or misleading. Critics say that when a person wants to get a comprehensive report of an event, he or she must turn to a newspaper; television news offers only simplified stories rather than denser and more detailed accounts.

Television news, argue the critics, concentrates mostly on stories of visual interest such as transport disasters or wars, leaving important but visually uninteresting stories such as government budget and legislation stories with little or no coverage. This leads to the claim that the selection of stories to be presented on television news tends less toward information and more toward entertainment. Thus, television news, according to this view, presents an image of the world that is quite subjective.

The reporting of political stories on television, in particular, is often criticised for failing to be either comprehensive or fair to the viewer. The main complaint is not that the news is politically biased, but that the limitations of the medium cause even important stories to be covered in as little as 60 seconds of broadcasting time. A politician is seen on the news to speak for between 10 and 30 seconds, for example, when in fact he or she may have been speaking for many times longer. Critics complain that viewers get used to seeing such abbreviated stories and thus become less inclined to watch longer, more thorough discussions of issues. Indeed, politicians, now long accustomed to speaking to television cameras, adjust their words to suit short news stories, because making long, elaborate arguments no longer works. Thus, television not only reports on politics, but has become a major influence on it.

Such views stand in contrast to those of US political scientist Ronald Butcher, who believes that television news is too complex and that it provides too much information. According to Butcher, the complexity of the presentation of television news programs prevents half of the audience from truly understanding many news stories. Moreover, it is assumed by news broadcasters that the viewer already knows much of the information that underlies particular stories. But this assumption, says Butcher, is inaccurate. The same can be said about how well viewers are able to interpret the importance of events.

Shoemaker and Lvov (1986) carried out research that showed that the ordinary television viewer 'fails to understand the main points in two-thirds of all major TV news stories'. Accounts of political events appear to offer the most difficulty for viewers because they make references to connected events and use terminology that only some people could readily comprehend. The researchers recommend that news programs make a greater effort to aid the viewer in understanding the events, no matter how many times the stories have been told before.

Regardless of how one feels about television news, research has left no doubt that it is the primary source of information for the vast majority of people in societies where television sets are widely available. In Australia, studies have shown that not only do most people get their news from television (see figure 1), but an increasing number of people regard television news as 'accurate and reliable'.

By what criteria, then, does the viewing public determine its level of confidence in television news?

In Australia, Johnson and Davis (1989) surveyed people's feelings about television news, as compared with newspapers and radio news. Although radio was believed by most people to be fastest in the delivery of the latest news, television news was rated first for such criteria as comprehensiveness of reporting and clarity of explanation. Similar research dating from 1966 put trust in newspapers ahead of television news for most of the same criteria.

The growing acceptance of television news as an information source that is reliable and trustworthy is reflected in the declining sales of newspapers in most modern societies. In Australia, newspaper circulation had dropped to 400 per thousand of population by 1992 from 576 per thousand some 26 years earlier, when the first television broadcasts were made in that country. Similar effects have been felt in the United States, where marketing surveys have revealed that working women — an important demographic group — have overwhelmingly embraced television news and rarely seek information from newspapers.

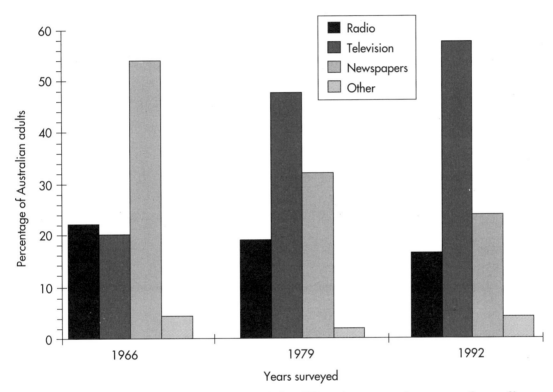

Figure 1: Survey question asked of Australian adults: 'What is your main source of news?'

Questions 29–34

*Complete the partial summary of 'Television News' below. Choose **NO MORE THAN THREE WORDS** from Reading Passage 3 for each answer. Write your answers in boxes 29–34 on your answer sheet.*

Critics of television news believe that newspapers are superior because they offer ... **(29)** ... versions of events. Indeed, news stories that cannot be presented in a ... **(30)** ... way are largely ignored by television news, which focuses primarily on events that have ... **(31)** .... However, research clearly shows that the public is turning increasingly to television as an information source, and that more people believe it offers better coverage of events in terms of such factors as ... **(32)** ... and ... **(33)** .... Indeed, one significant segment of the population moving away from printed news and toward televised news is ... **(34)** ....

Questions 35–38

'Television News' discusses several ways in which the TV viewer relates to news broadcasts. Decide which of the people (**A**, **B** or **C**) hold the views expressed below.

      A   Ronald Butcher

      B   Shoemaker and Lvov

      C   television news critics

Write your answers in boxes 35–38 on your answer sheet.

Example

The viewer is presented with too much information.

Answer: A

---

35.   The viewer is unlikely to seek comprehensive political coverage.

36.   The viewer is often unfamiliar with the background of certain news stories.

37.   The viewer may not understand stories because of unfamiliar political vocabulary.

38.   A story about a motor vehicle accident is more likely to be shown on television news than a story about the passing of a new law.

Questions 39–41

Complete the sentences below with words taken from Reading Passage 3. Use **NO MORE THAN ONE WORD** for each answer. Write your answers in boxes 39–41 on your answer sheet.

39.   The influence of television news has changed the way _____ express themselves.

40.   Australians rely on _____ for the most up-to-date news.

41.   The proportion of Australians who considered _____ their main source of news dropped by more than half from 1966 to 1992.

Practice IELTS Reading Subtest

Academic Module

PAPER FOUR

TIME ALLOWED: 1 hour
NUMBER OF QUESTIONS: 42

Instructions

WRITE ALL YOUR ANSWERS ON THE ANSWER SHEET

The test is in 3 sections:

– –	Reading Passage 1	Questions 1–12
– –	Reading Passage 2	Questions 13–28
– –	Reading Passage 3	Questions 29–42

Remember to answer all the questions. If you are having trouble with a question, skip it and return to it later.

---

*You are advised to spend about 15 minutes on **Questions 1–12**, which are based on Reading Passage 1.*

Of Ducks and Duck Eggs

For people who like to keep poultry, ducks offer certain advantages over hens. Ducks are immune to some common diseases found in hens and are less vulnerable to others. Some breeds of duck produce bigger eggs than hens. In addition, ducks lay eggs over a longer season than do hens.

Poultry keepers with gardens have less to worry about if they keep ducks rather than hens because the former are less apt to dig up plants and destroy roots. While both hens and ducks benefit the garden by eating pests, hens are known to damage herb and grass beds. Ducks, on the other hand, will search for insects and snails more carefully. Only very delicate plants are at risk from the broad, webbed feet of ducks.

Like all waterbirds, ducks need access to water, and duck keepers typically provide this by building a pond. Something this large is not absolutely necessary, however; ducks need only to be able to dip their heads in the water to keep their nostrils clean.

If a pond is provided, though, it is important to keep ducklings away from it until they are old enough to withstand the cool temperature of the water — about eight weeks.

When keeping ducks, one has to consider just how many the land will support. Generally the rule is 100 ducks per half hectare. If more than this proportion is introduced, there is a risk of compacting the soil, which can lead to muddy conditions for long periods as the rain is not easily absorbed into the ground.

While ducks offer many advantages over hens, they must be given a greater quantity of food, especially if regular eggs are desired. An adult duck will eat between 170 and 200 grams of food a day. If the ducks have access to grass and a pond, they will be able to find for themselves approximately 70 per cent of their daily dietary requirements in warmer months but less than half that in colder times. Therefore, it is important that they be fed enough food, such as grain, every day.

Experienced duck keepers raise ducklings every three years or so because it is after this period of time that ducks' egg-laying powers begin to seriously weaken. If the aim is to hatch ducklings, keepers should be aware that not all ducks make good mothers, and that certain breeds of duck appear to be worse than others. The poor mothers abandon their eggs a few days after laying them. A sure way of making sure the rejected eggs hatch is to place them next to chicken eggs under a hen.

The eggs of ducks as food for humans have a mixed reputation. This is because of a number of cases of salmonella food poisoning in Europe in the 1970s. Although it was never conclusively shown that duck eggs were to blame, the egg-eating public stopped buying and many duck egg producers went bankrupt. Indeed, there is a risk of salmonella poisoning when ducks lay their eggs in damp conditions, such as on ground that is constantly wet, but the same can be said for the eggs of hens. And commercial duck egg production in France and England, where the outbreaks of salmonella poisoning took place, followed the same standards as those used in the hen egg industry, which experienced no salmonella problems. (Storage of eggs, whether those of hen or duck, can also be a factor in contamination. Studies have found that bacterial growth reaches potentially dangerous levels at storage temperatures of 5°C or greater.)

The salmonella scare was over by the early 1980s, but, at least in smaller markets like Australia and New Zealand, few producers wished to risk investment in ducks for fear of problems. No large-scale commercial duck egg production exists in these countries. It has thus been left to small producers, and, more commonly, home duck keepers.

---

poultry: farm birds (e.g. chickens, geese, ducks)

Questions 1–6

Classify the characteristics listed below as belonging to:

        D   Ducks

        H   Hens

        or

        NI   if there is no information in the reading passage.

Write the appropriate letters in boxes 1–6 on your answer sheet.

Example	
more vulnerable to illness	*Answer:* H

1.   more eggs per week

2.   lengthier laying period

3.   less likely to uproot plants

4.   dangerous to grass

5.   eat more grain

6.   better mothers

Complete the partial summary below. Choose **ONE** *or* **TWO** *words from the passage for each answer. Write your answers in boxes 7–10 on your answer sheet.*

To prevent their ... **(7)** ... from getting dirty, ducks should have access to water. This may be provided by building a pond, but ducklings under ... **(8)** ... of age should be prevented from entering it because of the ... **(9)** ... of the water. If too many ducks are kept on a plot of land, the soil may eventually become ... **(10)** ... as a result of compaction. For this reason, it is advised that one limits the number of ducks per half hectare of land to 100.

Questions 11 and 12

Choose the appropriate letters **(A–D)** *and write them in boxes 11–12 on your answer sheet.*

11.   Salmonella food poisoning ...

      A   resulted from consumption of duck eggs.

      B   created difficulties for the duck egg business.

      C   occurred all over Europe.

      D   was found in both duck and hen eggs.

12.   Duck eggs ...

      A   have been produced in large quantities in New Zealand since the early 1980s.

      B   are more at risk of salmonella contamination than hen eggs.

      C   may be contaminated when laid in wet conditions.

      D   should be kept at 5°C to prevent contamination.

READING PASSAGE 2

You are advised to spend about 20 minutes on **Questions 13–28**, *which are based on Reading Passage 2.*

Questions 13–17

The Reading Passage 'Job Sharing' has 6 sections, A–F. Choose the most suitable headings for sections A, C, D, E and F from the list of headings at the top of the next page. Write the appropriate numbers **(i–x)** *in boxes 13–17 on your answer sheet.*

N.B.: There are more headings than sections so you will not use all of them. You may use any of the headings more than once.

13.   Section A

Example	
Section B	*Answer:* **iii**

14.   Section C

15.   Section D

16.   Section E

17.   Section F

Job Sharing

<u>Section A</u>

Job sharing refers to a situation in which two people divide the responsibility of one full-time job. The two people willingly act as part-time workers, working enough hours between them to fulfil the duties of a full-time worker. If they each work half the hours of the job, for example, they each receive 50 per cent of the job's wages, its holidays and its other benefits. Of course, some job sharers take a smaller or larger share of the responsibilities of the position, receiving a lesser or greater share of the benefits.

Job sharing differs from conventional part-time work in that it is mainly (although not exclusively) occurring in the more highly skilled and professional areas, which entail higher levels of responsibility and employee commitment. Until recently, these characteristics were not generally seen as compatible with anything less than full-time employment. Thus, the demands of job sharing are reciprocated by better pay and conditions and, ideally, more satisfaction than conventional part-time work.

<u>Section B</u>

Job sharing should not be confused with the term *work sharing*, which pertains to increasing the number of jobs by reducing the number of hours of each existing job, thus offering more positions to the growing number of unemployed people. Job sharing, by contrast, is not designed to address unemployment problems; its focus, rather, is to provide well-paid work for skilled workers and professionals who want more free time for other pursuits.

(*continued*)

Section C

As would be expected, women comprise the bulk of job sharers. A survey carried out in 1988 by Britain's Equal Opportunities Commission (EOC) revealed that 78 per cent of sharers were female, the majority of whom were between the ages of 20 and 40 years of age. Subsequent studies have come up with similar results. Many of these women were re-entering the job market after having had children, but they chose not to seek part-time work because it would have meant reduced wages and lower status. Job sharing also offered an acceptable transition back into full-time work after a long absence.

Section D

Although job sharing is still seen as too radical by many companies, those that have chosen to experiment with it include large businesses with conservative reputations. One of Britain's major banks, the National Westminster Bank, for example, offers a limited number of shared positions intended to give long-serving employees a break from full-time work. British Telecom, meanwhile, maintains 25 shared posts because, according to its personnel department, 'Some of the job sharers might otherwise have left the company and we are now able to retain them.' Two wide-ranging surveys carried out in the country in 1989 revealed the proportion of large and medium-sized private-sector businesses that allow job sharing to be between 16 and 25 per cent. Some 78 per cent of job sharers, however, work in public-sector jobs.

Section E

The types of jobs that are shared vary but include positions that involve responsibility for many sub-ordinates. Research into shared senior management positions suggests that even such high-pressure work can be shared between two people with little adjustment, provided the personalities and temperaments of the sharers are not vastly different from one another. A 1991 study of employees working under supervisory positions shared by two people showed that those who prefer such a situation do so for several reasons. Most prevalent were those who felt there was less bias in the evaluation of their work because having two assessments provided for a greater degree of fairness.

Section F

The necessity of close cooperation and collaboration when sharing a job with another person makes the actual work quite different from conventional one-position, one-person jobs. However, to ensure a greater chance that the partnership will succeed, each person needs to know the strengths, weaknesses and preferences of his or her partner before applying for a position. Moreover, there must be an equitable allocation of both routine tasks and interesting ones. In sum, for a position to be job-shared well, the two individuals must be well matched and must treat each other as equals.

Questions 18–22

*Complete the notes below for SECTION A. Choose **ONE** or **TWO WORDS** from the section for each answer. Write your answers in boxes 18–22 on your answer sheet.*

JOB SHARING
Common job sharing areas:

- highly skilled   *(Example)*

- ... **(18)** ...

Job sharing requires a greater degree of:

- ... **(19)** ...

- ... **(20)** ...

Benefits of job sharing over part-time work:

- ... **(21)** ...

- better conditions

- ... **(22)** ...

Questions 23–27

Do the following statements reflect the claims of the writer in Reading Passage 2? In boxes 23–27 write:

YES   *if the statement reflects the claims of the writer*
NO   *if the statement contradicts the writer's claims*
NOT GIVEN   *if there is no information about this in the passage.*

23. The majority of male job sharers are between 20 and 40 years of age.

24. Job sharers have no intention of later resuming full-time work.

25. Employers may allow job sharing to keep or attract good workers.

26. Fewer job sharers are employed in the private sector than in the public sector.

27. Most employees prefer to work under a shared supervisory position.

Question 28

*Choose the appropriate letter **A–D** and write it in box 28 on your answer sheet.*

28.   What is the main aim of the writer of 'Job Sharing'?

       A   to encourage employers to allow more job sharing

       B   to introduce the reader to the concept of job sharing

       C   to advise people who wish to try job sharing

       D   to discuss the implications of job sharing for industry

READING PASSAGE 3

*You are advised to spend about 25 minutes on **Questions 29–42**, which are based on Reading Passage 3 (next page).*

Question 29

*From the list below choose the most suitable title for the whole of Reading Passage 3. Write the appropriate letter **A–D** in box 29 on your answer sheet.*

       A   The Growing Incidence of Malaria

       B   The Worldwide Spread of Malaria

       C   Malaria Prevention Using Vaccines

       D   The Elimination of the Malaria Parasite

(Untitled)

The renewed spread of malaria in recent years, particularly in parts of sub-Saharan Africa, has been a cause of great concern to health workers and officials around the world. The global health community was once confident that the disease had been brought under control, with many successes in ridding large areas of malaria over the previous decades, but now increasingly large numbers of people are dying from the mosquito-borne ailment. Forty per cent of the world's population live in areas that are infected with malaria, and each year brings approximately 270 million new cases. Table 1 summarises recent distribution by geographic area.

The resurgence of malaria is occurring in several parts of the world. However, it is most acute in Africa, south of the Sahara Desert, where according to a 1993 World Health Organisation (WHO) report, between 1.4 and 2.8 million people, half of them children, now die each year from the disease. This is triple the annual number of people in the same region who die of AIDS. Actual numbers of malaria deaths may be even larger because the symptoms, such as chronic fever, are often mistaken for other, unrelated illnesses, such as influenza or pneumonia.

Table 1: Annual distribution of malaria infection, approximate, selected regions

	Sub-Saharan Africa	Southeast Asia	Indian subcontinent	South America	Northeast Asia
New cases (average per year)	135 million	66 million	46 million	17 million	6 million
of which children (average per year)	48 million	23 million	19 million	5.1 million	1.7 million
Deaths (average per year)	2.1 million	360 000	320 000	110 000	57 000

Incidences of cerebral malaria, which is caused by *Plasmodium falciparum*, the more dangerous of the two main malaria parasites, have been responsible for the growing number of fatalities in East Africa since the late 1980s. When treatment using chloroquine, which in many cases is not even effective, is not available, victims of cerebral malaria may survive as little as 24 hours.

In the 1950s, subtropical regions in the United States, southern Europe and elsewhere were sprayed with DDT, which eliminated the malaria parasite where used appropriately but resulted in resistant mosquitoes where sprayed too often. In other parts of the world at this time, chloroquine was introduced as a means of preventing infection, and it was thought to be effective in bringing down the number of malaria cases until the 1970s, when chloroquine-resistant strains of the parasite began to appear. The resistance kept getting stronger as time went on, and in some areas, such as Malawi and Kenya, malaria is now no longer preventable with commonly used drugs.

Increasing urbanisation is also responsible for the renewed spread of malaria in Africa. Because the parasite is more commonly found in rural areas where mosquitoes can breed in large numbers, people who are raised there have a significantly higher immunity to it than those reared in the towns and cities. Indeed, 5 per cent of children in the countryside die of malaria, and the many who survive it go on to become adults with a high degree of natural resistance. This is not the case with people living in urban areas; when such people go to visit relatives in the countryside, they are at much higher risk of contracting malaria.

Health workers, discouraged by the diminishing effectiveness of malarial drugs, are seeking to promote physical barriers to infection rather than chemical ones. The concept of mosquito nets hung over beds to keep mosquitoes away is certainly not new, but recent efforts to improve them have led to some success in protecting people from malaria. In experiments in Gambia, the number of children dying from malaria has dropped 50 per cent since using nets soaked in insecticide. To remain effective, the nets need to be resoaked only twice a year, and no drugs need to be taken for prevention. The nets provide additional benefits to the families who use them in that they prevent other types of irritating insects from getting too close.

Whether or not mosquito nets would be effective on a large scale remains to be seen, as conditions vary from place to place. Some users complain it is too hot under the nets to be able to sleep. Furthermore, their cost limits the number of people who can take advantage of them.

Thus the search for a vaccine for malaria continues. Manuel Patarroyo, a medical researcher from Colombia, stated in 1993 that he had been successful in trying a new vaccine on some 20 000 people in South America. Similar testing of the vaccine is being done in Africa, but health officials there are not convinced it will be effective because the rate at which new cases of malaria develop is many times higher than that in South America.

Although not a vaccine, *arthemeter*, derived from the Chinese herb *qinghao*, appears to offer an effective way of protecting people from malaria parasites. It proved to have tripled the effectiveness of chloroquine in research carried out in 1993 along the border of Thailand and Cambodia, an area not unlike sub-Saharan Africa in the strength of the parasite's resistance to conventional malarial drugs. There are plans for the new drug to be produced in China and marketed internationally by a French pharmaceutical company.

Questions 30–35

Use the information in Reading Passage 3 to indicate the relationship between the two items given for each question below. Classify them as:

  A   if there is a positive correlation

  B   if there is a negative correlation

  C   if there is little or no correlation

  D   if there is no information.

*Write the appropriate letters **A–D** in boxes 30–35 on your answer sheet.*

Example		
number of new malaria cases	number of malaria deaths	*Answer:* A

30.	malaria growth rate	incidence of influenza
31.	chloroquine used in 1950s	number of new malaria cases
32.	amount of chloroquine taken per day	effectiveness against disease
33.	resistance of parasite	number of new malaria cases
34.	growth of cities	number of new malaria cases
35.	use of soaked mosquito nets	number of new malaria cases

Questions 36–38

*Choose ONE phrase **A–H** from the list below to complete each key point. Write the appropriate letters **A–H** in boxes 36–38 on your answer sheet.*

The information in the completed sentences should be an accurate summary of points made by the writer.

*N.B.: There are more phrases **A–H** than sentences so you will not use them all. You may use any phrase more than once.*

36.   Malaria infection ...

37.   Arthemeter ...

38.   Use of DDT ...

A	has spread to 40 per cent of the population.
B	is preventable without the need for drugs.
C	has not been recorded in northeast Asia.
D	is especially effective in aiding victims of *Plasmodium falciparum*.
E	effectively rid parts of the world of the malaria parasite.
F	has been found to be effective in South America.
G	is claimed to be better at fighting infection than chloroquine.
H	is limited to malaria prevention.

Questions 39–42

*Answer each of the following questions using **NUMBERS** or **NO MORE THAN TWO WORDS** taken from Reading Passage 3. Write your answers in boxes 39–42 on your answer sheet.*

39.   Approximately how many children contract malaria each year in sub-Saharan Africa?

40.   Identify ONE symptom of malaria as discussed in the passage.

41.   Identify ONE country in which conventional drugs are no longer effective in preventing malaria.

42.   Identify ONE problem with the use of mosquito nets.

Practice IELTS Reading Subtest

Academic Module

PAPER FIVE

TIME ALLOWED: 1 hour
NUMBER OF QUESTIONS: 38

Instructions

WRITE ALL YOUR ANSWERS ON THE ANSWER SHEET

The test is in 3 sections:

– –   Reading Passage 1   Questions 1–13

– –   Reading Passage 2   Questions 14–28

– –   Reading Passage 3   Questions 29–38

Remember to answer all the questions. If you are having trouble with a question, skip it and return to it later.

READING PASSAGE 1

*You are advised to spend about 20 minutes on **Questions 1–13**, which are based on Reading Passage 1.*

Questions 1–4

Reading Passage 1 has 6 paragraphs.

*Choose the most suitable headings for paragraphs **C–F** from the list of headings below. Write the appropriate numbers (**i–ix**) in boxes 1–4 on your answer sheet.*

N.B.: There are more headings than paragraphs so you will not use all of them. You may use any of the headings more than once.

List of headings
i Uncertainty in categorisation
ii Preventing illegal immigration
iii Classification of border-crossers
iv Difficulty of changing one's immigration status
v Extent of error in card completion
vi Determining net flow of population
vii Reasons for high overall immigration
viii Computer-assisted measurement of illegal immigration
ix Improvements in departure and arrival cards

Example		
Paragraph B	*Answer:*	**iii**

1.   Paragraph C

2.   Paragraph D

3.   Paragraph E

4.   Paragraph F

Watching Freedonia's Borders

A Whenever a person enters or leaves the island nation of Freedonia, he or she must fill out an arrival or departure card. The data collected from the cards are entered into a computer database, known as the Inflow/Outflow Record (IOR). The Immigration Bureau uses the IOR to monitor changes in the population of Freedonia, which was estimated in 1994 to be 14.4 million people.

B The cards do more than just help count the number of people coming and going. The people who cross Freedonia's borders are put into one of several categories depending on how they fill out their card. The first category, labelled 'Category M' by the Immigration Bureau, is made up of people, usually tourists and business travellers from abroad, whose stay in Freedonia is shorter than 6 months. In 'Category N' are citizens and residents of Freedonia who go abroad for a similar period of time. 'Category P' includes foreigners who stay in Freedonia for a period greater than 6 months, while Freedonians who leave the country for more than 6 months are put in 'Category Q'. Then there are the people who migrate permanently to Freedonia, known as 'Category R', and those who permanently emigrate from the island state, who are placed in 'Category S'. Emigrants, it should be noted, are sometimes former immigrants to Freedonia.

C One problem with maintaining the IOR is that the departure and arrival cards ask for people's intentions, and intentions do not always become reality. Freedonia's population includes many people who originally entered the country on a temporary visa but who later applied for and were given permanent status; in this way, someone who was Category M becomes Category R. This is not too great a problem as changes in migration status inside the country can easily be tracked and entered into the IOR. It becomes difficult to make accurate categorisations, though, when Freedonians move overseas with plans to return — whether in less than 6 months or after a longer period — but do not, in fact, come back. Similarly, Freedonians who claim to be emigrating to other countries may change their minds and return to Freedonia.

D People may also make mistakes when filling out the cards. In 1984, a study was made of 21,730 arrival and departure cards filled out by people leaving from Freedonia's major airports and seaports. The study showed that one in five cards had errors. A total of 4008 passengers who were citizens of Freedonia mistakenly said that they were temporary entrants to Freedonia. Of these, 18 per cent were, in fact, emigrating or Category Q leavers. The study's most important finding was the lack of certainty expressed by departing Freedonians about when they planned to return to Freedonia. The arrival and departure cards were redesigned by the Immigration Bureau after the 1984 study, but while the new cards have been in use for over a decade, no new research has been done.

(*continued*)

E The unrecorded movements of people from one category to another make it hard to measure the flow of population, but it should be said that Freedonia is the only nation with high overall immigration that keeps reliable records of departures. In this way, the Immigration Bureau is able to keep track of departing native Freedonians as well as former settlers. By monitoring both immigration and emigration, the Bureau is able to maintain a record of net migration: the total gain or loss of people over a period of time. In other countries with high levels of immigration, the issue of net migration has often been neglected.

F One final benefit of the IOR is the help it gives in determining the level of illegal immigration to Freedonia. People who enter Freedonia saying they will stay in the country for under six months will appear automatically in the database as 'Category T' if they have not left the country after the end of that period. Unlike countries such as the United States that have little idea of the true extent of illegal immigration across their borders, Freedonia's Immigration Bureau has shown it is able to keep a fairly accurate count.

---

emigration: the act of leaving one country to settle in another

Questions 5–10

From the information in Reading Passage 1, classify the following individuals as:

M	for Category M
N	for Category N
P	for Category P
Q	for Category Q
R	for Category R
S	for Category S
T	for Category T

*Write the appropriate letters **M–T** in boxes 5–10 on your answer sheet.*

N.B.: There are more categories than individuals so you will not use them all. You may use the same category more than once.

5. Ms Y, an Australian, marries a Freedonian and decides to live permanently with her husband in Freedonia.

6. Mr U, a Freedonian citizen, leaves on a business trip and returns after four months.

7. Mr X, originally from France, migrated to Freedonia 15 years ago. He now decides to move back to France with no plans to return to Freedonia.

8. Ms W, a Freedonian university graduate, leaves Freedonia on a one-year, round-the-world ticket.

9. Mr Z, an Italian, was classified as Category M on arrival early last year. He is still in Freedonia but has made no effort to change his migration status.

10. Ms V, a United States citizen, spends her yearly two-week vacation in Freedonia.

Question 11

*Complete the sentence below with words taken from Reading Passage 1. Use **NO MORE THAN TWO WORDS**. Write your answer in box 11 on your answer sheet.*

11.   Quite a few Freedonians incorrectly completed their arrival and departure cards by saying they were

_____ .

Questions 12 and 13

Reading Passage 1 mentions THREE types of records that Freedonia keeps better than do some other countries. ONE of them is 'departures'. What are the other TWO?

*Use **NO MORE THAN TWO WORDS** for each answer. Write one answer in box 12 and the other in box 13 of your answer sheet.*

READING PASSAGE 2

*You are advised to spend about 20 minutes on **Questions 14–28**, which are based on Reading Passage 2.*

Tea Tree Oil

The first mention of 'tea tree oil' was documented when Joseph Banks, a botanist, sailed with Captain James Cook to the Australian continent in the late 18th century. Banks observed the native Aborigines collecting the leaves of a tree, now known scientifically as *Melaleuca alternifolia*. They used the leaves, after boiling them, to heal a variety of external skin problems. Banks also learned that by boiling the leaves he could produce a tasty brew similar to lemon tea. Thereafter, he referred to this particular species of trees generically as the 'tea tree', a name commonly applied to it today.

Little was known by the European settlers of the beneficial effects of tea tree oil until around 1924, when A. R. Penfold, of the Sydney Technological Museum, began research into why and how this unique oil was able to produce such positive results. After several years of evaluation, he concluded that tea tree oil was one of the most effective natural antiseptics and fungicides known to exist at that time.

In fact, the natural healing qualities of tea tree oil were found to be so effective that during World War II the Australian government sent all available supplies to Australian troops serving in the Pacific. The oil was used as a first line of defence against such skin problems as burns, cuts, abrasions, insect bites, sunburn, and a broad spectrum of other external fungal and bacterial problems. It was so important to the overall war effort that anyone involved in either the harvesting or the processing of tea tree oil was exempt from active military service.

Melaleuca trees grow naturally only in a limited area along the north coast of the state of New South Wales. This is an area known to be extremely rugged and swampy for many months of the year. Because of these conditions, harvesting the oil from the natural stands of Melaleuca trees was often very difficult. This, plus the tremendous increase in demand brought about by the war, led scientists to begin searching for alternative methods and products that could effectively solve some of those same problems, and that could be produced

(continued)

more efficiently and economically. The advent of penicillin around this time was one result of this search, and tea tree oil was all but forgotten by the rest of the world. It has only been during the past couple of decades, with a return in many societies to natural products, that tea tree oil is again becoming widely known.

Tea trees have narrow leaves and paper-like barks, and seldom exceed 20 feet in height. They are very hardy trees; some trees along the Bungwalyn Creek have been harvested for more than 60 years and still flourish. For years, the tea tree was considered a nuisance by farmers because of the difficulty of their eradication in the process of clearing the ground for farming. With recent broad recognition of the oil's properties, however, several commercial plantations with trees numbering into the millions have been established in anticipation of large-scale demand.

Contrary to initial assumptions, tea tree oil is not taken from the sap of the tree. It is, in fact, derived from the 'fat' of the tree. Because these trees grow in an area of Australia where climatic conditions vary greatly, they fortify themselves by storing up essential nutrients in small nodules found in their leaves and stems. In the past, the leaves and stems were cut and placed in crude containers of water. Building a fire

Melaleuca alternifolia

under the containers would heat the water, producing steam, which made the nodules burst, thus releasing the oil into the water. Through a primitive system of gravity separation, the oil would flow into a collection vat while the water would be released to the ground. The net result would be pure, unadulterated tea tree oil.

Today, through the introduction of huge plantations and mechanisation, essentially the same process is accomplished on a larger scale. However, much care is taken not to disturb the natural growth and delicate balance nature has prescribed to create tea tree oil.

Because each tree is unique, the quality of the oil extracted will vary from tree to tree. In fact, shifts in climate, soil and other environmental conditions may cause the quality of the oil from the same tree to fluctuate from year to year. Pure tea tree oil is composed of 48 chemical compounds that work together synergistically to create this highly effective oil. If one of these compounds is removed from the oil, the overall effectiveness is diluted.

Questions 14–18

Choose ONE phrase A–G to complete each key point below. Write the appropriate letters A–G in boxes 14–18 on your answer sheet.

The information in the completed sentences should be an accurate summary of points made by the writer.

N.B.: There are more phrases A–G than sentences so you will not use them all. You may use any phrase more than once.

14.   The Aborigines . . .

15.   Joseph Banks . . .

16.   A. R. Penfold . . .

17.   Australian soldiers . . .

18.   Tea tree oil producers . . .

A	. . . knew little about the beneficial effects of the oil of the Melaleuca tree.
B	. . . gave Melaleuca the name 'tea tree'.
C	. . . used the extracted oil of the Melaleuca for skin problems.
D	. . . helped in the wartime search for alternatives to tea tree oil.
E	. . . did not have to serve in the military during World War II.
F	. . . studied tea tree oil and its healing qualities.
G	. . . used the leaves of the Melaleuca tree to treat skin problems.

Questions 19–24

*Complete the sentences below with words taken from Reading Passage 2. Use **NO MORE THAN ONE WORD** for each blank space. Write your answers in boxes 19–24 on your answer sheet.*

19.   It is difficult to harvest oil from naturally grown Melaleuca trees because they are found in a
        _____ and _____ location.

20.   Interest in tea tree oil declined after the development of _____ .

21.   The Melaleuca tree's ability to withstand repeated harvesting over time is such that some trees are
        reported to have produced oil for more than _____ years.

22.   Until recently, farmers viewed the Melaleuca tree as a _____ .

23.   Tea tree oil was originally thought to come from the _____ of the Melaleuca tree.

24.   Oil from the same tree may vary with changes in _____ and _____ .

The diagram below shows how tea tree oil was extracted before the introduction of modern techniques.

Complete the diagram. Choose **ONE** *or* **TWO** *words from the passage for each answer. Write your answers in boxes 25–28 on your answer sheet.*

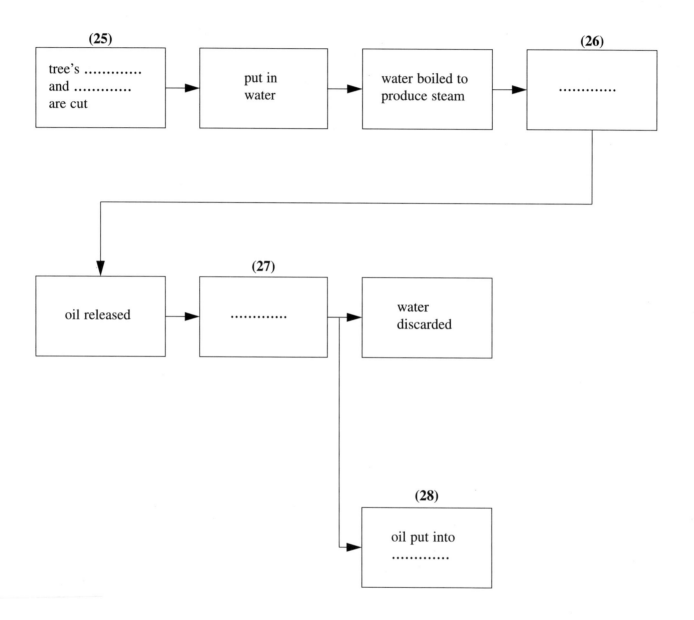

(25)

tree's ....
and ....
are cut

put in
water

water boiled to
produce steam

(26)

....

oil released

(27)

....

water
discarded

(28)

oil put into
....

READING PASSAGE 3

*You are advised to spend about 20 minutes on **Questions 29–38**, which are based on Reading Passage 3.*

The Dangers of Air-conditioning

About two-thirds of the world's population is expected to live in cities by the year 2020 and, according to the United Nations, approximately 3.7 billion people will inhabit urban areas some ten years later. As cities grow, so do the number of buildings that characterise them: office towers, factories, shopping malls and high-rise apartment buildings (see figure 1). These structures depend on artificial ventilation systems to keep clean and cool air flowing to the people inside. We know these systems by the term 'air-conditioning'.

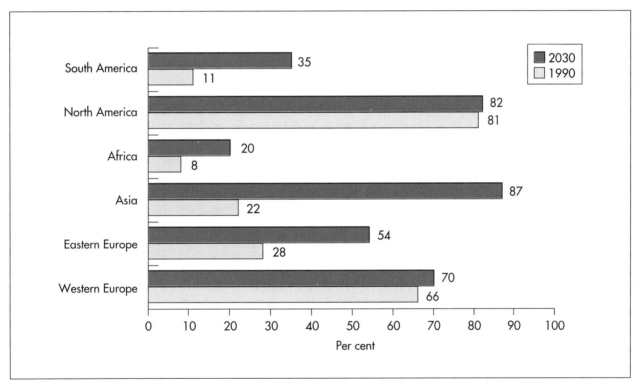

Figure 1: Percentage of population living or working in air-conditioned environments, 1990 and 2030 (projected).

Although many of us may feel air-conditioners bring relief from hot, humid or polluted outside air, they pose many potential health hazards. Much research has looked at how the circulation of air inside a closed environment — such as an office building — can spread disease or expose occupants to harmful chemicals.

One of the more widely publicised dangers is that of Legionnaire's disease, which was first recognised in the 1970s. This was found to have affected people in buildings with air-conditioning systems in which warm air pumped out of the system's cooling towers was somehow sucked back into the air intake, in most cases owing to poor design. This warm air was, needless to say, the perfect environment for the rapid growth of disease-carrying bacteria originating from outside the building, where it existed in harmless quantities. The warm, bacteria-laden air was combined with cooled, conditioned air and was then circulated around various parts of the building. Studies

(continued)

showed that even people outside such buildings were at risk if they walked past air exhaust ducts. Cases of Legionnaire's disease are becoming fewer with newer system designs and modifications to older systems, but many older buildings, particularly in developing countries, require constant monitoring.

Cigarette smoke is also carried from room to room by some air-conditioning systems, bringing with it the attendant risks of passive smoking. The past few years have seen a lot of studies into passive smoking — the smoke breathed in by non-smokers living or working near smokers. In Japan, a survey of medical records showed that women whose husbands do not smoke are half as likely to acquire lung cancer as those who are married to smokers. Research into passive smoking in an office setting demonstrated similar risks for non-smokers working for many years next to smokers. Smoky air circulated by the air-conditioning system of the average office, according to an Australian study, caused non-smokers to breathe in the equivalent of three cigarettes in one day of work.

The ways in which air-conditioners work to 'clean' the air can inadvertently cause health problems, too. One such way is with the use of an electrostatic precipitator, which removes dust and smoke particles from the air. What precipitators also do, however, is emit large quantities of positive air ions into the ventilation system. A growing number of studies show that overexposure to positive air ions can result in headaches, fatigue and feelings of irritation.

Large air-conditioning systems add water to the air they circulate by means of humidifiers. In older systems, the water used for this process is kept in special reservoirs, the bottoms of which provide breeding grounds for bacteria and fungi that can find their way into the ventilation system. The risk to human health from this situation has been highlighted by the fact that the immune systems of approximately half of workers in air-conditioned office buildings have developed antibodies to fight off the organisms found at the bottom of system reservoirs. Chemical disinfectants, called 'biocides', which are added to reservoirs to make them germ-free, are dangerous in their own right in sufficient quantities, as they often contain compounds such as pentachlorophenol, which is strongly linked to abdominal cancers.

Finally, it should be pointed out that the artificial climatic environment created by air-conditioners can also adversely affect us. In a natural environment, whether indoor or outdoor, there are small variations in temperature and humidity. Indeed, the human body has long been accustomed to these normal changes. In an air-conditioned living or work environment, however, body temperatures remain well under 37°C, our normal temperature. This leads to a weakened immune system and thus greater susceptibility to diseases such as colds and flu.

---

duct: a tube or pipe through which air travels
humidifier: device to make air humid
reservoir: a tank used for storing water

Questions 29–31

*Using **NO MORE THAN TWO WORDS**, answer the following questions. Write your answers in boxes 29–31 on your answer sheet.*

29. Which part of the world will experience the smallest growth in air-conditioning between 1990 and 2030?

30. Which part of the world will experience the largest growth in air-conditioning between 1990 and 2030?

31. In which part of the world is Legionnaire's disease more likely to occur?

Questions 32 and 33

The diagram below shows how Legionnaire's disease is spread.

*Complete the diagram by identifying objects 32 and 33. Choose **TWO** words from the passage for each answer. Write your answers in boxes 32–33 on your answer sheet.*

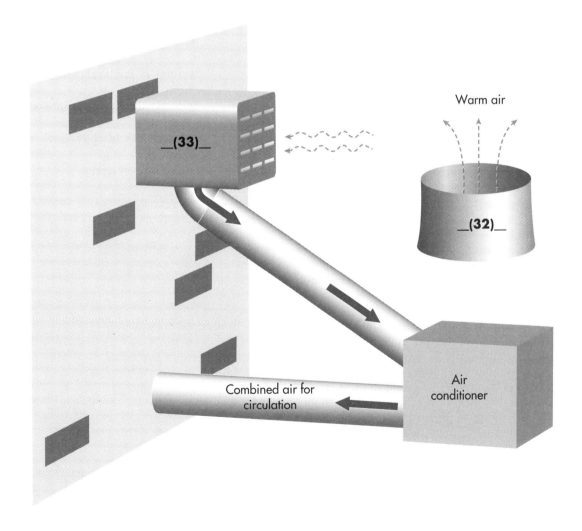

Warm air

__(33)__

__(32)__

Combined air for circulation

Air conditioner

Questions 34–38

Using the information in Reading Passage 3, indicate the relationship between the two items given for each question below by marking on your answer sheet:

PC   if there is a positive correlation

NC   if there is a negative correlation

L/N   if there is little or no correlation

NI   if there is no information

*Write your answers (**PC, NC, L/N** or **NI**) in boxes 34–38 on your answer sheet.*

Example

smoking in office   risk of cancer to non-smokers

Answer: PC

---

34.   level of smoke in air   incidence of headaches

35.   use of electrostatic precipitator   feelings of calm/relaxation

36.   use of humidifier   antibody development in workers

37.   use of certain biocides in humidifiers   potential risk of abdominal cancers

38.   natural indoor temperature fluctuation   risk to human health

Practice IELTS Reading Subtest

Academic Module

PAPER SIX

TIME ALLOWED: 1 hour
NUMBER OF QUESTIONS: 38

Instructions

WRITE ALL YOUR ANSWERS ON THE ANSWER SHEET

The test is in 3 sections:

– –	Reading Passage 1	Questions 1–10
– –	Reading Passage 2	Questions 11–25
– –	Reading Passage 3	Questions 26–38

Remember to answer all the questions. If you are having trouble with a question, skip it and return to it later.

*You should spend about 15 minutes on **Questions 1–10**, which are based on Reading Passage 1.*

Question 1

1.　　The author of 'Keeping Cut Flowers' believes flower care is dependent on three main factors. One of them is **temperature**. What are the other TWO?

Write your answer in box 1 on your answer sheet.

Keeping Cut Flowers

While everybody enjoys fresh cut flowers around their house, few people know how to keep them for as long as possible. This may be done by keeping in mind a few simple facts.

An important thing to remember about cut flowers is that they are sensitive to temperature. For example, studies have shown that cut carnations retain their freshness eight times longer when kept at 12°C than when kept at 26°C. Keeping freshly harvested flowers at the right temperatures is probably the most important aspect of flower care.

Flowers are not intended by nature to live very long. Their biological purpose is simply to attract birds or insects, such as bees, for pollination. After that, they quickly wither and die. The process by which flowers consume oxygen and emit carbon dioxide, called *respiration*, generates the energy the flower needs to give the flower its shape and colour. The making of seeds also depends on this energy. While all living things respire, flowers have a high level of respiration. A result of all this respiration is heat, and for flowers, the level of heat relative to the mass of the flower is very high. Respiration also brings about the eventual death of the flower, thus the greater the level of respiration, the sooner the flower dies.

How, then, to control the rate at which flowers die? By controlling respiration. How is respiration controlled? By controlling temperature. We know that respiration produces heat, but the reverse is also true. Thus by maintaining low temperatures, respiration is minimised and the cut flower will age more slowly. (Tropical flowers are an exception to this rule; they prefer warmer temperatures.)

Cooler temperatures also have the benefit of preserving the water content of the flower, which helps to slow down ageing as well. This brings us to another important aspect of cut flower care: humidity. The average air-conditioned room has a relative humidity of 65 per cent, which contributes to greater water loss in the flower. Flowers are less likely to dry out if humidity levels are 90–95 per cent, but this may be unrealistic unless you live in the tropics or subtropics.

Yet another vital factor in keeping cut flowers is the quality of the water in which they are placed. Flowers find it difficult to 'drink' water that is dirty or otherwise contaminated. Even when water looks and smells clean, it almost certainly contains bacteria and fungi that can endanger the flowers. To rid the water of these unwanted germs, household chlorine bleach can be used in small quantities. It is recommended that 15 drops of chlorine bleach (at 4 per cent solution) be added to each litre of water. The water and solution should also be replaced each day.

When buying cut flowers, look for ones that have not been kept (by the flower shop) in direct sunlight or strong wind. If the flowers are not freshly harvested, ask whether they have been stored in a refrigerated coolroom.

Questions 2–4

*Complete the sentences below with words taken from Reading Passage 1. Use **NO MORE THAN ONE WORD** or **NUMBER** for each blank. Write your answers in boxes 2–4 on your answer sheet.*

2.   A difference of 14°C can extend the life of carnations by up to _____ times.

3.   _____ and _____ are two aspects of a flower's appearance that depend on respiration.

4.   Respiration is also necessary for the flowers to produce _____ .

Questions 5–8

*Complete the flow chart below. Choose **NO MORE THAN THREE WORDS** from the passage for each answer. Write your answers in boxes 5–8 on your answer sheet.*

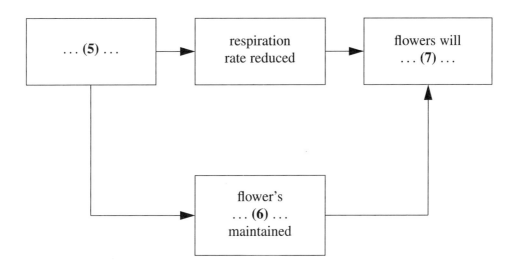

The above diagram does not apply to ... **(8)** ... flowers.

Questions 9 and 10

*Using **NO MORE THAN TWO WORDS**, answer the following questions. Write your answer in boxes 9–10 on your answer sheet.*

9.   What product does the author suggest using to help protect cut flowers?

10.   The author identifies two natural elements that shopkeepers should keep from flowers. Name one of these.

*You should spend about 25 minutes on **Questions 11–25**, which are based on Reading Passage 2.*

Literacy in Freedonia's Prisons

In 1993, the Government of Freedonia's National Prisons Directorate (NPD) carried out a research project to investigate the extent of literacy in Freedonia's prison population.

The notion that prisoners are poor readers and writers seems to be questioned very little by the public despite the lack of hard evidence to support such a view. The media, in particular, continue to portray prisoners as illiterate and generally poorly educated. Freedonia's leading daily newspaper, *The Freedonian*, for example, frequently makes such statements as 'Freedonia's jails are full of people who can't read!' (4 May 1992). But the media are not the only ones who are critical. Research into attitudes of prison officials shows that they, too, hold that prisoners are poor readers (McDonnell 1989). Overseas studies have also been influential in strengthening this view. For example, a survey of Canadian prisoners by Kohl in 1987 revealed a literacy rate ranging from 15 per cent to 55 per cent, while an Australian study of the same year showed similar results. To add to the general criticism, Freedonia's criminologists are beginning to suggest that crime is a product of illiteracy (Bass 1988; Katz & Wallport 1989). The NPD commissioned its study to compare prisoner literacy with that of the general public to see how Freedonian prisoners actually conform to these perceptions.

The study, carried out by the Literacy Institute of the Freedonian National University, took as samples 200 male prisoners from Yaxchilan Men's Correctional Institute and 150 female prisoners from Monambak Women's Prison. The prisoners were each made to work through a series of activities designed to assess performance in three separate literacy areas. The three areas included what the study termed 'X-literacy', which is the ability to correctly fill out forms or follow written directions; 'Y-literacy', the comprehension of reading passages; and 'Z-literacy', which calls for correct interpretation of text that is primarily number-based. This latter skill often includes some calculation. All activities were identical to those used in a national adult literacy survey carried out in 1990.

It was found that the prison population did, in fact, have a lower rate of X-literacy than the general population, but that the overall difference was slight. In an activity that had the prisoners complete mock job applications, for example, just 62 per cent of female and 60 per cent of male prisoners could correctly fill out the applications compared with 66 per cent in the national adult sample (see figure 1). Similar differences were found between general and prison populations in completing insurance applications, although it should be mentioned that individual differences in this task were great.

There were activities in which prisoners were noticeably weaker, however. In one activity, the proportion of male prisoners who could correctly identify the main and secondary points of newspaper articles was 54 per cent, compared with 64 per cent of the general public. Interestingly, female prisoners, with 61 per cent, were much closer to the national average for this activity. Prisoners, again more noticeably males, also did significantly worse in keeping a running total of a bank account, a quantitative task of relative complexity.

But, importantly, both male and female prisoners outperformed the national adult sample in other activities; in one, far fewer general adults than prisoners could correctly interpret train timetables, while in identifying directions on medical prescriptions, both male and female prisoners were marginally better than their counterparts on the other side of the prison fence.

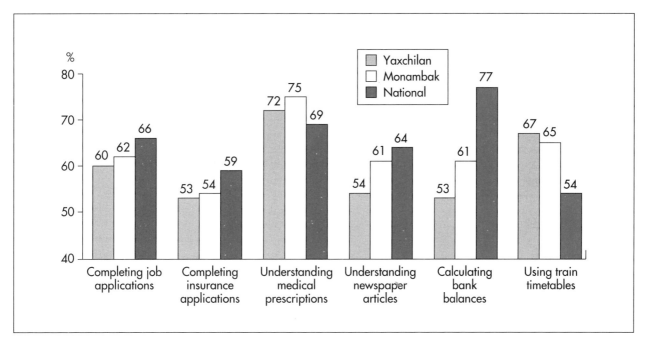

Figure 1: Percentage correct on assorted literacy tasks

The results show that prisoners and the general adult population, seen from an overall perspective, are on an equivalent literacy level. Certainly, prisoners appear to display weaknesses in particular literacy areas, but if the results accurately reflect the prison population as a whole, it would be inaccurate and hence inappropriate to conclude that prisoners are the worse readers and writers. The study should not be taken to suggest that there are no literacy problems among prisoners, however, because while prisoners may be no worse off than the general adult public, the general adult public cannot be said to perform very well in any of the literacy tasks. Indeed, in commenting on the results of the NPD study, Wallport (1994) wrote, 'It seems our initial assessment of literacy among prisoners was not incorrect. Where we were mistaken was in how we viewed the skill levels of the general public.'

---

literacy: the ability to read and write
mock: not real

Questions 11–13

The author of Reading Passage 2 mentions several influences on how prisoner literacy is generally viewed. One of these influences is '**Freedonia's criminologists**'. Identify **THREE** other influences.

*Using **NO MORE THAN TWO WORDS** for each answer, write the three influences separately in boxes 11–13 on your answer sheet.*

Questions 14–18

Below is a list of the materials used in assessing the three literacy areas in the NPD study. Complete the list. Choose ONE or TWO WORDS from the passage for each answer. Write your answers in boxes 14–18 on your answer sheet.

MATERIALS USED IN:

<u>X-literacy activities</u>

- ... **(14)** ...
- ... **(15)** ...

> *Example*
>
> - medical prescriptions

<u>Y-literacy activities</u>

- ... **(16)** ...

<u>Z-literacy activities</u>

- ... **(17)** ...
- ... **(18)** ...

Questions 19–21

Complete the partial summary below. Choose your answers A–F from the list below the summary and write them in boxes 19–21 on your answer sheet.

N.B.: There are more phrases than spaces so you will not use them all. You may use any of the phrases more than once.

In comparing the NPD study's findings with that of a similar study of the general adult population in 1990, it was shown that the general adult population was most proficient at correctly ... E ... (*Example*). The largest percentage-point difference between female prisoners and male prisoners was found in ... **(19)** ... . Male prisoners scored higher than their female counterparts in ... **(20)** ... , and ranked between female prisoners and the general public in ... **(21)** ... .

A	completing an employment application
B	completing an insurance application
C	following medical prescription directions
D	comprehending newspaper articles
E	balancing bank accounts
F	using train timetables

Questions 22 and 23

In analysing the results of the study, the Literacy Institute determined that, owing to the sample sizes, differences in scores of 3 percentage points or lower could not be considered significant.

22.   How many of the literacy activities in the NPD study showed a difference between male and female prisoners that was significant?

23.   How many of the literacy activities showed a difference between female prisoners in the NPD study and the general adult public in the national adult study that was NOT significant?

*Write the correct **NUMBERS** in boxes 22 and 23 on your answer sheet.*

Questions 24 and 25

*Choose the appropriate letters **A–D** and write them in boxes 24–25 on your answer sheet.*

24.   In setting up its study, the NPD wished to ...

      A   see if prisoner illiteracy matched public perceptions.

      B   show that prisoner literacy levels are not lower than those of the general adult public.

      C   identify areas in which prisoners need literacy training.

      D   show that popular perceptions of prisoner literacy are not correct.

25.   The NPD study suggests that ...

      A   it is inaccurate to say prisoners have a low literacy level.

      B   prisoners compare favourably with the general adult population.

      C   neither prisoner literacy nor general adult literacy is very satisfactory.

      D   prisoners are worse readers and writers than general adults.

*You are advised to spend about 20 minutes on **Questions 26–38**, which are based on Reading Passage 3.*

Wild Foods of Australia

More than 120 years ago, the English botanist J. D. Hooker, writing of Australian edible plants, suggested that many of them were 'eatable but not worth eating'. Nevertheless, the Australian flora, together with the fauna, supported the Aboriginal people well before the arrival of Europeans. The Aborigines were not farmers and were wholly dependent for life on the wild products around them. They learned to eat, often after treatment, a wide variety of plants.

The conquering Europeans displaced the Aborigines, killing many, driving others from their traditional tribal lands, and eventually settling many of the tribal remnants on government reserves, where flour and beef replaced nardoo and wallaby as staple foods. And so, gradually, the vast store of knowledge, accumulated over thousands of years, fell into disuse. Much was lost.

However, a few European men took an intelligent and even respectful interest in the people who were being displaced. Explorers, missionaries, botanists, naturalists and government officials observed, recorded and, fortunately in some cases, published. Today, we can draw on these publications to form the main basis of our knowledge of the edible, natural products of Australia. The picture is no doubt mostly incomplete. We can only speculate on the number of edible plants on which no observation was recorded.

Not all our information on the subject comes from the Aborigines. Times were hard in the early days of European settlement, and traditional foods were often in short supply or impossibly expensive for a pioneer trying to establish a farm in the bush. And so necessity led to experimentation, just as it must have done for the Aborigines, and experimentation led to some lucky results. So far as is known, the Aborigines made no use of *Leptospermum* or *Dodonaea* as food plants, yet the early settlers found that one could be used as a substitute for tea and the other for hops. These plants are not closely related to the species they replaced, so their use was not based on botanical observation. Probably some experiments had less happy endings; L. J. Webb has used the expression 'eat, die and learn' in connection with the Aboriginal experimentation, but it was the successful attempts that became widely known. It is possible the edibility of some native plants used by the Aborigines was discovered independently by the European settlers or their descendants.

Explorers making long expeditions found it impossible to carry sufficient food for the whole journey and were forced to rely, in part, on food that they could find on the way. Still another source of information comes from the practice in other countries. There are many species from northern Australia that occur also in South-East Asia, where they are used for food.

In general, those Aborigines living in the dry inland areas were largely dependent for their vegetable foods on seed such as those of grasses, acacias and eucalypts. They ground these seeds between flat stones to make a coarse flour. Tribes on the coast, and particularly those in the vicinity of coastal rainforests, had a more varied vegetable diet with a higher proportion of fruits and tubers. Some of the coastal plants, even if they had grown inland, probably would have been unavailable as food since they required prolonged washing or soaking to render them non-poisonous; many of the inland tribes could not obtain water in the quantities necessary for such treatment. There was also considerable variation in the edible plants available to Aborigines in different latitudes. In general, the people who lived in the moist tropical areas enjoyed a much greater variety than those in the southern part of Australia.

With all the hundreds of plant species used for food by the Australian Aborigines, it is perhaps surprising that only one, the Queensland nut, has entered into commercial cultivation as a food plant. The reason for this probably does not lie with an intrinsic lack of potential in Australian flora, but rather with the lack of exploitation of this potential. In Europe and Asia, for example, the main food plants have had the benefit of many centuries of selection and hybridisation, which has led to the production of forms vastly superior to those in the wild. Before the Europeans came, the Aborigines practised no agriculture and so there was no opportunity for such improvement, either deliberate or unconscious, in the quality of the edible plants.

Since 1788, there has, of course, been opportunity for selection of Australian food plants that might have led to the production of varieties that were worth cultivating. But Australian plants have probably 'missed the bus'. Food plants from other regions were already so far in advance after a long tradition of cultivation that it seemed hardly worth starting work on Australian species. Undoubtedly, the native raspberry, for example, could, with suitable selection and breeding programs, be made to yield a high-class fruit; but Australians already enjoy good raspberries from other areas of the world and unless some dedicated amateur plant breeder takes up the task, the Australian raspberries are likely to remain unimproved.

And so, today, as the choice of which food plants to cultivate in Australia has been largely decided, and as there is little chance of being lost for long periods in the bush, our interest in the subject of Australian food plants tends to relate to natural history rather than to practical necessity.

---

edible: fit to be eaten
botany: the study of plants

Questions 26–32

Do the following statements reflect the claims of the writer in Reading Passage 3? In boxes 26–32 write:

YES   *if the statement reflects the writer's claims*
NO   *if the statement contradicts the writer*
NOT GIVEN   *if there is no information about this in the passage.*

26.   Most of the pre-European Aboriginal knowledge of wild foods has been recovered.

27.   There were few food plants unknown to pre-European Aborigines.

28.   Europeans learned all of what they knew of edible wild plants from Aborigines.

29.   *Dodonaea* is an example of a plant used for food by both pre-European Aborigines and European settlers.

30.   Some Australian food plants are botanically related to plants outside Australia.

31.   Pre-European Aboriginal tribes closer to the coast had access to a greater variety of food plants than tribes further inland.

32.   Some species of coastal food plants were also found inland.

Questions 33–35

*Choose the appropriate letters (**A–D**) and write them in boxes 33–35 on your answer sheet.*

33.   Wallaby meat ...

      A   was regularly eaten by Aborigines before European settlement.

      B   was given by Aborigines in exchange for foods such as flour.

      C   was a staple food on government reserves.

      D   was produced on farms before European settlement.

34.   Experimentation with wild plants ...

      A   depended largely on botanical observation.

      B   was unavoidable for early settlers in all parts of Australia.

      C   led Aborigines to adopt *Leptospermum* as a food plant.

      D   sometimes had unfortunate results for Aborigines.

35.   Wild plant use by Aborigines ..

      A   was limited to dry regions.

      B   was restricted to seed.

      C   sometimes required the use of tools.

      D   was more prevalent in the southern part of Australia.

Questions 36–38

*Complete the partial summary below. Choose **ONE** or **TWO** words from the passage for each answer. Write your answers in boxes 36–38 on your answer sheet.*

Despite the large numbers of wild plants that could be used for food, only one, the ... **(36)** ..., is being grown as a cash crop. Other edible plants in Australia, however much potential they have for cultivation, had not gone through the lengthy process of ... **(37)** ... that would allow their exploitation, because Aborigines were not farmers. Thus species such as the ... **(38)** ..., which would be an agricultural success had it not had to compete with established European varieties at the time of European settlement, are of no commercial value.

Practice Writing *Papers*

The six Practice Writing Papers that follow should be attempted under test conditions. No dictionary or other reference book may be used and time limits must be strictly kept.

Write your answers to Tasks 1 and 2 on separate sheets of paper.

You may wish to compare your answers with sample answers given on pages 148–153.

PRACTICE WRITING PAPER ONE

WRITING TASK 1

You should spend about 20 minutes on this task.

Eating sweet foods produces acid in the mouth, which can cause tooth decay. (High acid levels are measured by low pH values.)

Describe the information below and discuss the implications for dental health.

You should write at least 150 words.

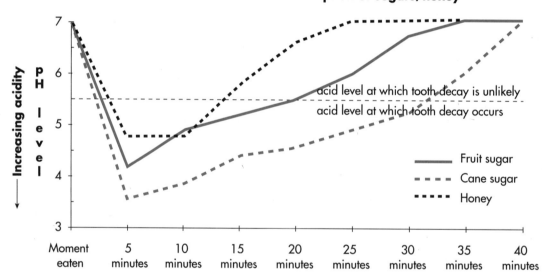

Acid level in mouth from consumption of sugars/honey

acid level at which tooth decay is unlikely

acid level at which tooth decay occurs

Fruit sugar
Cane sugar
Honey

Increasing acidity

PH level

Moment eaten — 5 minutes — 10 minutes — 15 minutes — 20 minutes — 25 minutes — 30 minutes — 35 minutes — 40 minutes

Time elapsed after eating sugar/honey

WRITING TASK 2

You should spend about 40 minutes on this task.

Present a written argument or case to an educated reader with no specialist knowledge of the following topic.

> **In some countries the average worker is obliged to retire at the age of 50, while in others people can work until they are 65 or 70. Meanwhile, we see some politicians enjoying power well into their eighties. Clearly, there is little agreement on an appropriate retirement age.**
>
> **Until what age do you think people should be encouraged to remain in paid employment?**
>
> **Give reasons for your answer.**

You should write at least 250 words.

You should use your own ideas, knowledge and experience and support your arguments with examples and relevant evidence.

PRACTICE WRITING PAPER TWO

WRITING TASK 1

You should spend about 20 minutes on this task.

The graphs below show the numbers of male and female workers in 1975 and 1995 in several employment sectors of the republic of Freedonia.

Write a report for a university teacher describing the information shown.

You should write at least 150 words.

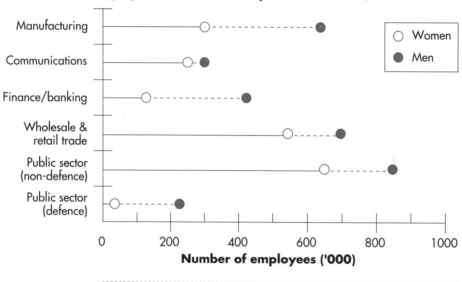

Employment in Freedonia by sex in 6 sectors, 1975

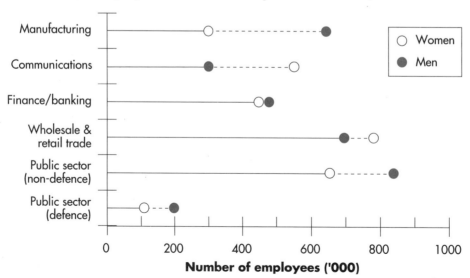

Employment in Freedonia by sex in 6 sectors, 1995

WRITING TASK 2

You should spend about 40 minutes on this task.

Present a written argument or case to an educated reader with no specialist knowledge of the following topic.

> **Going overseas for university study is an exciting prospect for many people. But while it may offer some advantages, it is probably better to stay home because of the difficulties a student inevitably encounters living and studying in a different culture.**
>
> **To what extent do you agree or disagree with this statement?**
>
> **Give reasons for your answer.**

You should write at least 250 words.

You should use your own ideas, knowledge and experience and support your arguments with examples and relevant evidence.

PRACTICE WRITING PAPER THREE

WRITING TASK 1

You should spend about 20 minutes on this task.

> **The diagram below shows the typical stages of consumer goods manufacturing, including the process by which information is fed back to earlier stages to enable adjustment.**
>
> **Write a report for a university lecturer describing the process shown.**

You should write at least 150 words.

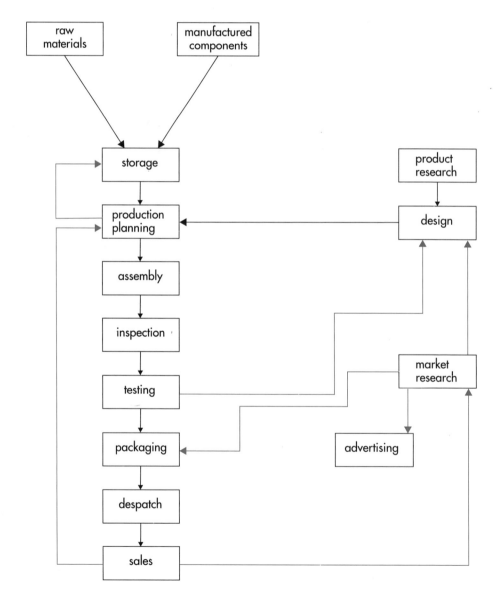

Flow of manufacturing process

Flow of information feedback

WRITING TASK 2

You should spend about 40 minutes on this task.

Present a written argument or case to an educated reader with no specialist knowledge of the following topic.

> **Many people believe that women make better parents than men and that this is why they have the greater role in raising children in most societies. Others claim that men are just as good as women at parenting.**
>
> **Write an essay expressing your point of view.**
>
> **Give reasons for your answer.**

You should write at least 250 words.

You should use your own ideas, knowledge and experience and support your arguments with examples and relevant evidence.

PRACTICE WRITING PAPER FOUR

WRITING TASK 1

You should spend about 20 minutes on this task.

> The chart below shows the sleep patterns of people in five different occupations according to a Canadian study.
>
> Write a report for a university lecturer, describing the information below. Give possible reasons for the differences.

You should write at least 150 words.

Occu-pation	6–7 pm	7–8 pm	8–9 pm	9–10 pm	10–11 pm	11–12 pm	12–1 am	1–2 am	2–3 am	3–4 am	4–5 am	5–6 am	6–7 am	7–8 am	8–9 am	9–10 am	10–11 am	11–12 am	12–1 pm	1–2 pm	2–3 pm	3–4 pm	4–5 pm	5–6 pm
Student						■	■	■	■	■	■	■	■											
Truck driver	■													■	■								■	■
Full-time mother					■					■	■										■			
Business executive						■	■	■	■		■													
Doctor								■	■		■	■	■											

□ awake   ■ asleep

WRITING TASK 2

You should spend about 40 minutes on this task.

Present a written argument or case to an educated reader with no specialist knowledge of the following topic.

The mass media, including television, radio and newspapers, have great influence in shaping people's ideas.

To what extent do you agree or disagree with this statement?

Give reasons for your answer.

You should write at least 250 words.

You should use your own ideas, knowledge and experience and support your arguments with examples and relevant evidence.

PRACTICE WRITING PAPER FIVE

WRITING TASK 1

You should spend about 20 minutes on this task.

The table below shows social and economic indicators for four countries in 1994, according to United Nations statistics.

Describe the information shown below in your own words. What implications do the indicators have for the countries?

You should write at least 150 words.

Indicators	Canada	Japan	Peru	Zaire
Annual income per person (in $US)	11 100	15 760	160	130
Life expectancy at birth	76	78	51	47
Daily calorie supply per person	3 326	2 846	1 927	1 749
Adult literacy rate (%)	99	99	68	34

WRITING TASK 2

You should spend no more than 40 minutes on this task.

Write an essay for a university teacher on the following topic.

> **'Telecommuting' refers to workers doing their jobs from home for part of each week and communicating with their office using computer technology. Telecommuting is growing in many countries and is expected to be common for most office workers in the coming decades.**
>
> **How do you think society will be affected by the growth of telecommuting?**

You should write at least 250 words.

You may wish to discuss this in terms of your own society, or human societies in general.

You should use your own ideas, knowledge and experience and support your arguments by examples and by relevant evidence.

PRACTICE WRITING PAPER SIX

WRITING TASK 1

You should spend no more than 20 minutes on this task.

> The diagram below shows the average hours of unpaid work per week done by people in different categories. (Unpaid work refers to such activities as childcare in the home, housework and gardening.)
>
> Describe the information presented below, comparing results for men and women in the categories shown. Suggest reasons for what you see.

You should write at least 150 words.

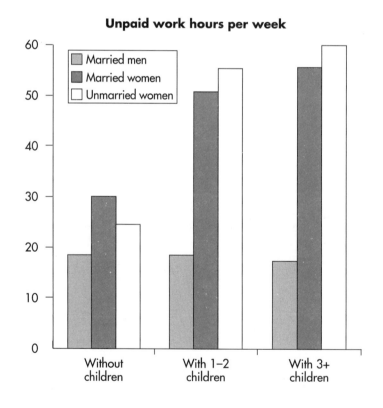

Unpaid work hours per week

Legend:
- Married men
- Married women
- Unmarried women

WRITING TASK 2

You should spend about 40 minutes on this task.

Write an essay for a university lecturer on the following topic.

> **The rising levels of congestion and air pollution found in most of the world's cities can be attributed directly to the rapidly increasing number of private cars in use. In order to reverse this decline in the quality of life in cities, attempts must be made to encourage people to use their cars less and public transport more.**
>
> **Discuss possible ways to encourage the use of public transport.**

You should write at least 250 words.

You should use your own ideas, knowledge and experience and support your arguments with examples and relevant evidence.

Answers

 Interpreting your practice test results

Although the Listening and Reading practice papers contained in this book have undergone trialling and statistical analysis, we make no claim that the results you attain on them will match your results on the real IELTS test. Thus, instead of providing a band score, we offer the following rough guide as a means of interpreting your test scores. Keep in mind that the level of difficulty (and the number of questions) varies slightly across the tests contained in this book.

LISTENING

Your score

31–40	A score in this range indicates you are likely to do well to very well in the actual IELTS Listening Module.
17–30	A score in this range indicates you will need to concentrate more on your listening skills in order to obtain adequate results in the actual IELTS Listening Module.
0–16	A score in this range indicates you are unlikely to obtain adequate results in the actual IELTS Listening Module if attempted any time soon. We recommend you make a serious effort to improve your listening skills.

READING

Your score

29–40	A score in this range indicates you are likely to do well to very well in the actual IELTS Reading Module.
16–28	A score in this range indicates you will need to concentrate more on your reading skills in order to obtain adequate results in the actual IELTS Reading Module.
0–15	A score in this range indicates you are unlikely to obtain adequate results in the actual IELTS Reading Module if attempted any time soon. We recommend you make a serious effort to improve your reading skills.

Answer keys

Note the following symbols used in the answer keys.

( )	for words that are not a necessary part of the answer
/	between alternative words or phrases within one answer
//	between acceptable alternative answer forms
;	between words/phrases that are both needed to answer a set of questions
AND	between words/phrases that must both be included for an answer to be correct

Practice Listening Paper One

1. D
2. C
3. C
4. √ will join
5. √ will join
6. √ will not join AND (going to) Canada // overseas
7. √ will not join AND (going to) Queensland
8. Ballantyne (*must be spelled correctly*)
9. 7743 2129
10. American Express
11. $175
12. E
13. H
14. B
15. 70/seventy
16. 13/thirteen
17. A
18. D
19. C
20–21. G; B (*either order*)

22. 30/thirty million
23. second/2nd
24. below 600 metres
25. instant (coffee)
26. blended (coffee)
27. Uganda
28. √ Brazil, √ USA, √ UK (*must be all THREE*)
29. √ Italy
30. √ France, √ Germany, √ Japan (*must be all THREE*)
31. (the) United Nations
32. Freezing (weather)
33. B
34. content
35. process
36. B
37. E
38. A
39. C
40. E
41. D

Practice Listening Paper Two

1. history
2. B
3. F
4. D
5. D
6. C
7. 9/nine
8. Wednesday
9. Tuesday
10. 3/three
11. 10/ten
12. 1100
13. northeast
14. rectangle/rectangular//square
15. warm
16. northwest
17. 2/two million
18. beach(es)
19. 250 000
20. hot springs//mineral baths//bushwalking//mountains
21. southwest
22. Spanish
23. wine
24. 2/two
25. 1/one
26. 4/four
27. D
28. A
29. C
30. Japan
31. fashionable
32. liver
33. cigarette smoke/smoking
34. formal introduction(s)//formal situation(s)
35. not interested
36. G
37. C
38. D
39. H
40. A
41. F
42. E

Practice Listening Paper Three

1. B
2. A
3. D
4. C
5. C
6. √ Greek salad (*Sareena*)
7–9. √ Chicken sandwich (*Sareena*)
   √ Chicken sandwich (*Vincent*)
   √ Onion soup (*Vincent*)
10. A
11. C
12. rental prices//rent
13. $650
14. 350–650
15. northern Chapmanville//north
16. river
17. bay
18. insects//mosquitoes
19–20. pollution//polluted (bay); (airport) noise//airport (*any order*)
21. trains AND buses
22. buses
23. quality
24. cullet
25. 25/twenty-five
26. beer bottles
27. 30/thirty
28. standardisation
29. shopkeepers//shops
30. return
31. 10/ten
32. transport//transportation//transporting
33–36. A; C; E; H (*any order*)
37. √ (school graduation) AND √ (spouse leaves work)
38. √ (pregnancy)
39. √ (divorce)
40. C
41. communicating less//less communication//talking less//less talk
42. less energy//little energy//feeling tired
43. sleeping//falling asleep

Practice Reading Paper One

1. Cooke and/& Wheatstone
2. Western Union (Company)
3. Reis
4. telephone
5. harmonic telegraph
6. C
7. A
8. E
9. D
10. B
11. fragile//awkward (to use)//difficult to transport//expensive (to build)
12. rail station(s)
13. musical tones
14. harmonic telegraph
15. B
16. D
17. F
18. A
19. E
20. F
21. D
22. E
23. B
24. A
25. C
26. avoidant
27. anxious–ambivalent
28. avoidant
29. ii
30. vii
31. ix
32. v
33. iv
34–35. 911 emergency system; (police) computer (systems) (*either order*)
36. Yes
37. Yes
38. Yes
39. Not given
40. No
41. Yes
42. Not given

Practice Reading Paper Two

1. C
2. E
3. F
4. A
5. 12
6. 11
7. (15–) 19
8. 20//20–24//24
9. suburban areas
10. D
11. L/N
12. PC
13. NI
14. NC
15. NC
16. Yes
17. Not given
18. No
19. No
20. Yes
21. Not given
22. Yes
23. iii
24. x
25. ix
26. i
27. ii
28. vii
29–32. A; C; E; G (*any order*)
33–34. low wages; surplus labour (*either order*)
35. small businesses
36. on foot
37. private automobiles

Practice Reading Paper Three

1. A
2. (southwestern) United States AND China//(China's) Xinjiang (Province) (*must have both*)
3. Australia//New Zealand//North America//Western Europe (*any THREE*)
4–7. A; D; E; G (*any order*)
8. 35/thirty-five (%)/(percent)
9. (commercially sold) timber//brick (products)
10. passive solar capacity//(walls) store heat
11. cement//sand//straw//cow dung (*any TWO*)
12. coatings//paints
13. cracks//(early) deterioration
14. E
15. O
16. B
17. A
18. Agfitz (1973)
19. Agfitz (1972a)
20. Haldern &/and Matthews (1969)
21. Namimitsu &/and Matthews (1971)
22. Wilson (1976)
23. Vilberberg &/and Zhou (1991)
24. Agfitz (1972b)
25. Not given
26. Yes
27. Yes
28. No
29. comprehensive//denser//(more) detailed
30. simplified
31. visual interest//entertainment
32–33. comprehensiveness (of reporting); clarity (of explanation)
34. working women
35. C
36. A
37. B
38. C
39. politicians
40. radio
41. newspapers

Practice Reading Paper Four

1. NI
2. D
3. D
4. H
5. NI
6. H
7. nostrils
8. 8/eight weeks
9. (cool) temperature
10. muddy
11. B
12. C
13. v
14. i
15. ii
16. x
17. vii
18. professional
19–20. responsibility; (employee) commitment (*either order*)
21–22. better pay; more satisfaction (*either order*)
23. Not given
24. No
25. Yes
26. Yes
27. Not given
28. B
29. A
30. C
31. B
32. D
33. A
34. A
35. B
36. B
37. G
38. E
39. 48 million
40. chronic fever
41. Malawi//Kenya
42. too hot//cost

Practice Reading Paper Five

1. i
2. v
3. vi
4. viii
5. R
6. N
7. S
8. Q
9. T
10. M
11. temporary entrants
12–13. net migration; illegal immigration (*either order*)
14. G
15. B
16. F
17. C
18. E
19. rugged *AND* swampy (*either order*)
20. penicillin
21. 60/sixty
22. nuisance
23. sap
24. climate *AND* soil (*either order*)
25. leaves *AND* stems (*either order*)
26. nodules burst
27. gravity separation
28. collection vat
29. North America
30. Asia
31. developing countries
32. cooling towers
33. air intake
34. NI
35. NC
36. PC
37. PC
38. L/N

Practice Reading Paper Six

1. humidity *AND* water quality (*either order*)
2. 8/eight
3. shape *AND* colour (*either order*)
4. seeds
5. controlling temperature//maintaining low temperatures//cooler temperatures
6. water content
7. age (more) slowly
8. tropical
9. chlorine bleach
10. direct sunlight//strong wind
11–13. (the) media; prison officials; overseas studies (*any order*)
14–15. job applications; insurance applications (*either order*)
16. newspaper articles
17–18. train timetables; bank accounts (*either order*)
19. E
20. F
21. C
22. 2/two
23. 1/one
24. A
25. C
26. No
27. Not given
28. No
29. No
30. Yes
31. Yes
32. Not given
33. A
34. D
35. C
36. Queensland nut
37. selection//hybridisation//improvement//breeding
38. (native) raspberry

Sample answers for Writing Papers

Practice Writing Paper One

Task 1

Anyone who has visited a dentist has been told that eating excessive amounts of sweets risks harming the teeth. This is because sweets lower pH levels in the mouth to dangerous levels.

When the pH level in the mouth is kept above 5.5, acidity is such that teeth are unlikely to be in danger of decay. Sweet foods, however, cause pH in the mouth to drop for a time, and the longer pH levels remain below 5.5, the greater the opportunity for decay to occur.

By comparing fruit sugar, cane sugar and honey, which are all common ingredients of sweet foods, we find that cane sugar lowers pH levels for the longest period, thus producing the greatest risk of the three. Approximately five minutes after consuming cane sugar, pH levels drop to as little as pH 3.5. They then begin to rise slowly, but do not rise above pH 5.5 until at least 30 minutes have elapsed. By contrast, fruit sugar, which causes the mouth's acidity to fall to just above pH 4, poses a danger for a shorter period: tooth decay is unlikely 20 minutes after consumption. Honey appears an even less risky substance. Though acidity falls to about pH 4.75 within five minutes of consumption, it returns to above pH 5.5 in under fifteen minutes.

The implications, then, are that people who insist on eating sweet foods should be aware of the ingredients, and that fruit sugar or honey appear preferable to cane sugar. (242 words)

Task 2

Mandatory retirement age varies from society to society, perhaps a reflection of economics, population pressures or simply value systems. Indeed, retirement at 50 can probably be as easily justified as that at 70. It is my belief, however, that the longer an able person is allowed to work, the better for both the individual worker and the employer.

Chronological age is not always a true indicator of ability. While some 65-year-olds may not perform as well as they did in their past, many workers at this age do just as well or better than they used to. People's suitability for a position should be a reflection of their performance in the job, rather than the number of wrinkles or grey hairs they have. Employers concerned about the increasing age of their employees need only observe their work records. Those doing poorly may be asked to retire, but those as yet unaffected by age should stay on. Indeed, it would appear economical for an organisation to retain its older employees when possible rather than spend time and money on training new workers.

Remaining in one's job for as long as one is able makes sense as life expectancies increase around the world. As people live longer, they are longer able to contribute to society in the form of meaningful work. But they are also in need of income for a longer period, so a mandatory retirement age of 55 for someone who is statistically likely to live to 77 becomes increasingly difficult to justify. At a time when populations are ageing, governments are less able to provide for their senior citizens, so by keeping able workers in paid employment for as long as is practicable, public expenditures are less strained.

Thus, workers who can still demonstrate their capacity to carry out their work should not be asked to retire simply because they have reached a certain age. Societies that insist on early retirement may do well to look again at their policies. (333 words)

Practice Writing Paper Two

Task 1

The two decades between 1975 and 1995 brought significant changes in the representation of women in Freedonia's work force, according to the graphs.

In 1975, for example, some 300 000 men and 250 000 women worked in the communications sector. Twenty years later, though the number of men remained unchanged, the number of women rose to 550 000.

A similar situation was seen in the wholesale and retail trade sector, where the number of women rose from about 550 000 in 1975 to almost 800 000 two decades later. The number of men in this sector remained stable over the period, at around 700 000.

Women also made gains in both the finance/banking industries and in the defence-related public sector. Whereas some 125 000 women worked in finance and banking institutions in 1975, the number increased to 450 000 by 1995. The number of men grew only marginally from 425 000 to 480 000 over the same period. In defence, the number of men declined from 225 000 to 200 000, while the number of women rose from 25 000 to over 100 000.

Two sectors that retained stable employment numbers for both men and women were manufacturing, which had about 300 000 women and 650 000 men in both surveyed years, and the public sector (non-defence), which employed 650 000 women and 850 000 men.

Thus, women appear to have made gains in the Freedonian work force but not at the expense of men.

(243 words)

Task 2

There is no doubt that going to study in a foreign country, with its different language and culture, can be a frustrating and sometimes painful experience. But while overseas study has its drawbacks, the difficulties are far outweighed by the advantages. Indeed, people who go abroad for study open themselves up to experiences that those who stay at home will never have.

The most obvious advantage to overseas university study is real-life use of a different language. While a person can study a foreign language in his or her own country, it cannot compare with constant use of the language in academic and everyday life. There is no better opportunity to improve second-language skills than living in the country in which it is spoken. Moreover, having used the language during one's studies offers a distinct advantage when one is applying for jobs back home that require the language.

On a university campus, the foreign student is not alone in having come from far away. He or she will likely encounter many others from overseas and it is possible to make friends from all around the world. This is not only exciting on a social level, but could lead to important overseas contacts in later professional life.

Finally, living and studying abroad offers one a new and different perspective of the world and, perhaps most important, of one's own country. Once beyond the initial shock of being in a new culture, the student slowly begins to get a meaningful understanding of the host society. On returning home, one inevitably sees one's own country in a new, often more appreciative, light.

In conclusion, while any anxiety about going overseas for university study is certainly understandable, it is important to remember that the benefits offered by the experience make it well worthwhile.

(301 words)

Practice Writing Paper Three

Task 1

Most consumer goods go through a series of stages before they emerge as finished products ready for sale.

Raw materials and manufactured components comprise the initial physical input in the manufacturing process. Once obtained, these are stored for later assembly. But assembly first depends upon the production planning stage, where it is decided how and in what quantities the stored materials will be processed to create sufficient quantities of finished goods. The production planning stage itself follows the requirements of the goods' design stage that proceeds from extensive research. After assembly, the products are inspected and tested to maintain quality control. Those units that pass the inspection and testing stages are then packaged, despatched and offered for sale in retail outlets. The level of sales, which is the end point of the manufacturing process, helps determine production planning.

A product's design is not only the result of product research, but is also influenced by testing and market research. If the testing stage (after assembly and inspection) reveals unacceptable problems in the finished product, then adjustments will have to be made to the product's design. Similarly, market research, which examines the extent and nature of the demand for products, has the role of guiding product design to suit consumer demands that may change with time. Market research, while influenced by product sales, also serves to foster future sales by devising suitable advertising for the goods.

Thus the reality of consumer goods manufacturing goes well beyond a simple linear production process.

(246 words)

Task 2

The view that women are better parents than men has shown itself to be true throughout history. This is not to say that men are not of importance in child-rearing; indeed, they are most necessary if children are to appreciate fully the roles of both sexes. But women have proven themselves superior parents as a result of their conditioning, their less aggressive natures and their generally better communication skills.

From the time they are little girls, females learn about nurturing. First with dolls and later perhaps with younger brothers and sisters, girls are given the role of carer. Girls see their mothers in the same roles and so it is natural that they identify this as a female activity. Boys, in contrast, learn competitive roles far removed from what it means to nurture. While boys may dream of adventures, girls' conditioning means they tend to see the future in terms of raising families.

Girls also appear to be less aggressive than boys. In adulthood, it is men, not women, who prove to be the aggressors in crime and in war. Obviously, in raising children, a more patient, gentle manner is preferable to a more aggressive one. Although there certainly exist gentle men and aggressive women, by and large, females are less likely to resort to violence in attempting to solve problems.

Finally, women tend to be better communicators than men. This is shown in intelligence tests, where females, on average, do better in verbal communication than males. Of course, communication is of utmost importance in rearing children, as children tend to learn from and adopt the communication styles of their parents.

Thus, while it is all very well to suggest a greater role for men in raising children, let us not forget that women are generally better suited to the parenting role.

(303 words)

Practice Writing Paper Four

Task 1

Differences in sleep patterns appear to reflect differences in individuals' occupations.

A Canadian study has pointed out, for example, that students typically sleep for a consecutive 8-hour period each night, from 11 p.m. to 7 a.m. This may be because the central activity in their lives, study, takes place in normal daylight hours. Similarly, business executives sleep consecutive hours, but perhaps because their jobs are especially busy and stressful they sleep for 6 hours on average, getting up around 5 a.m.

By contrast, truck drivers, probably because of their need to keep their trucks on the road over long periods, tend to sleep in two 3-hour blocks: one between 7 and 10 a.m. and another from 4 to 7 p.m. Another occupation associated with broken sleep schedules is that of doctors. They tend to retire to bed around 1 a.m. and start their day at 7 a.m., but may be woken up to deal with emergencies in the middle of the night. Finally, full-time mothers, especially those with young children, tend to sleep when their babies do. Typically, they will sleep from 10 p.m. and be awoken at 1 a.m. to comfort their babies for a couple of hours. They then go back to bed to wake at 6 a.m., but nap for two hours or so in the early afternoon.

Thus the influence on one's sleep pattern is worthy of consideration when choosing an occupation.

(239 words)

Task 2

The mass media have a powerful influence in shaping our lives. We have come to depend on them for information and entertainment, and in doing so we let them affect important aspects of our lives.

The undeniable usefulness of the media in almost instantly providing information about events around the world is largely taken for granted. But in our dependence on the media we have allowed them to mould our notions and opinions of events, places and people. Though few of us probably think about it, our conceptions of, say, our elected officials spring from television images and newspaper stories. Most of us will never meet prime ministers or presidents, but anyone who is regularly exposed to the media will have an opinion of them. When it is time to cast our vote, we will make our decision based on how the media portray the candidates. We are similarly swayed by coverage of wars. The media, representing the values of their owners, societies and governments, tend to report wars with a bias; which is the 'good' side and which the 'bad' is determined for us by reporters, editors and commentators, and sure enough the public begins to form opinions that reflect the coverage they see, hear and read in the major media.

The media are also influential in the way they facilitate the spread of culture and lifestyle. The so-called 'global youth culture', in which one finds young people around the world displaying a common interest in music, clothing styles and films, is an example of the media's enormous sway in this regard. A popular figure such as Michael Jackson would never be so well known were it not for the media's extensive reach into every society on the globe.

Thus I would argue that the mass media's influence is certainly great. Indeed, with technological advancements such as the Internet bringing even more forms of electronic media to our homes and workplaces, it is likely the media's influence will grow even stronger.

(333 words)

Practice Writing Paper Five

Task 1

A glance at four indicators of economic and social conditions in four countries, Canada, Japan, Peru and Zaire, in 1994 reflects the great differences that exist between wealthier and poorer nations.

The table shows that Japan and Canada had annual incomes of $15 760 and $11 100 per person, respectively. These figures were overwhelmingly greater than the corresponding figures of $160 in Peru and $130 in Zaire.

Health indicators, too, reflected overall levels of affluence in the four nations. Life expectancy at birth, for example, was higher among the more economically developed countries. Japan reported the highest life expectancy, 78. This was followed by Canada, 76; Peru, 51; and Zaire, 47. This suggests that richer societies are able to put more money into health care than poorer ones.

The number of calories consumed daily per person roughly followed the same ranking. Canadians each consumed some 3326 calories per day while the Japanese took 2846 calories. The corresponding figures for Peru and Zaire were 1927 and 1749, respectively.

Literacy rates among adults, too, were higher in wealthier countries, no doubt a reflection of ability to invest in education. Canada and Japan both reported literacy rates of 99 per cent, while Peru claimed 68 per cent. Zaire, the least economically developed of the four countries, had a literacy rate of 34 per cent.

The data appear to confirm the often cited link between national wealth and health and education standards.

(236 words)

Task 2

The spread of telecommuting is sure to have far-reaching effects on society. By itself, telecommuting refers to office workers spending much of their time working from home and using electronic technologies to communicate with their employers. The broader implications of telecommuting, however, may involve changes to corporate structure, workers' lifestyles and even urban planning.

The most obvious changes may be apparent in the 'normal' offices of companies, governments and other organisations. If even half the working week is spent telecommuting from home, then we would initially expect many empty desks in the office. As offices become smaller, workers coming in for the day would be expected to share desks with their absent colleagues. This, in turn, may affect the social atmosphere of an organisation, however, as less social contact with one's colleagues could harm morale and loyalty.

For the individual office worker, telecommuting would mean spending more time at home. For a parent with young children, this may be a blessing. Moreover, many telecommuters would be able to work the hours they wished: having a nap in the afternoon, for example, but working some hours in the evening. One substantial benefit for all telecommuting workers is that there will be no need to travel to work, allowing more free time.

The structure of urban life is also likely to be affected by telecommuting. We would expect to see fewer cars on the road during peak hours and, eventually, a smaller concentration of offices in cities' central business districts. In short, people will have less reason to travel to city centres from outlying areas. As more people work and live in the same location, shops and cultural events will likely be relocated out of the city centre.

In sum, telecommuting will serve to change not only the way we work but also the way we live.

(306 words)

Practice Writing Paper Six

Task 1

The diagram reveals that the hours per week spent in unpaid work are unequally distributed between men and women, and, to a lesser extent, between married and unmarried women.

In households without children, where the partners are married, women reportedly spend 30 hours per week doing housework, gardening etc. Men's contribution to these tasks averages a considerably lower 18 hours. When children enter the household, however, the inequality becomes even greater. In families of 1–2 children, men maintain approximately the same number of hours of unpaid work as in childless households, but the number of hours women work in the home rises to 52 per week — much of it, no doubt, due to childcare responsibilities. Interestingly, when there are 3 or more children, men are found to work even fewer hours. Whereas women's unpaid hours rise to approximately 56 per week, the corresponding figure for men, 16, represents a decrease.

Comparing women according to marital status, wedded childless women work about 5 more unpaid hours per week than their unmarried counterparts — perhaps explained by perceived marital obligations. In contrast, unmarried mothers, regardless of number of children, work an additional 4 hours per week compared with married mothers.

(193 words)

Task 2

Anyone who lives in a city is aware of the increasing number of cars on the road and the kinds of problems this creates: traffic jams, air pollution and longer commuting periods. As economies grow and access to cars spreads to increasing numbers of people, this trend is likely to worsen. The solution, it would seem, is for government to encourage the use of public transport in urban areas, thus decreasing dependence on the car.

One way to stimulate public transport use is to make private car use more expensive and inconvenient. The introduction of tolls along urban motorways has been successfully employed in many cities. Other such measures are high-priced permits for parking in urban areas and the restriction of parking to a limited number of cars. Faced with high costs or no place to park, commuters would perhaps be more willing to abandon their cars in favour of buses or trains.

There are also less punishing ways of spurring public transport use. The construction of free carparks at suburban train stations has proven successful in quite a number of countries. This allows commuters to drive part of the way, but take public transport into the central, most congested, urban areas.

Indeed, making public transport more comfortable and convenient should work to attract more commuters and decrease traffic congestion. Public transport that is convenient and comfortable retains its passengers, much like any business that satisfies its customers. The more commuters committed to taking public transport, the less congestion on city streets.

(253 words)

Tapescripts *for the*
Practice Listening Subtests

 Paper One

Section 1

ANNOUNCER: Listening Section 1. In a moment, you are going to hear a conversation between Claudia and Toshio, who are two overseas students in Australia. They are discussing plans to take a holiday after their studies finish. Before you listen, look at Questions 1 to 7. Note the examples that have been done for you.

(*Pause*)

As you listen to the first part of the conversation, answer Questions 1 to 7.

TOSHIO: Well, Claudia, our first semester at university is almost over. I can't wait for the holidays.

CLAUDIA: Me too, Toshio! Why don't we go somewhere far away and forget about lectures and essays and all that hard work.

TOSHIO: Sounds good to me. Now, how long will we have before we have to be back here on campus for the next semester?

CLAUDIA: We've got about six weeks, I think.

TOSHIO: How about if we go to the coast? It would be great to do some swimming and surfing.

CLAUDIA: The coast would be good. But let's look at our other options. There's the mountains. They're nice and cool at this time of year. And we can do some bush-walking. There's also the desert, which I really enjoyed last year.

TOSHIO: What about going to Sydney? I've never been there and they say it's a great city to visit. Lots of things to do there, I've heard.

CLAUDIA: I agree Sydney would be good but there are too many tourists there at this time of year. And I'd rather get away from buildings and cars. There are enough of those around here. I vote for the mountains.

TOSHIO: All right, then, let's do that. Now we have to decide where we're going to stay and how we're going to get there. Any suggestions?

CLAUDIA: Well, for places to stay, there are the usual places: motels, hotels, youth hostels. We could go camping, too.

TOSHIO: I'm afraid I'm not a very good camper, Claudia. I tend to feel a bit frightened sleeping outdoors. And the hassle of building fires and all the insects, and . . .

CLAUDIA: All right, all right. We'll forget about camping. Although I must admit it would've been my first choice. So what should we do?

TOSHIO: Well, since neither of us has a lot of money, I don't think a hotel or motel would be possible. How about a youth hostel?

CLAUDIA: I'd rather not go to a youth hostel, Toshio. They're certainly cheap, but you never get to be alone in those places; there's always a stranger in the next bed, and I hate sharing kitchens with people I don't know. No, I think we should find a small holiday house to rent. And if we get a few more friends to join us, it will be really cheap.

TOSHIO: I think your idea's spot on. But, who should we ask along? How about Peter? Do you think he'd want to join us?

CLAUDIA: I was just talking to him this morning and he said he was flying home to Hong Kong for a visit.

TOSHIO: Oh. Well, what about Maria and her boyfriend Gyorg? Oh, and David Wong might be interested. And his brother Walter is studying here, too. We can ask him.

CLAUDIA: Hang on, not so fast, please. I'm writing a list of people to ring. Let me think. We could ask Jennifer, too. I don't think she has any plans. And Michael Sullivan, perhaps, too. I think I'll just ring them all now.

ANNOUNCER: After ringing their friends, Claudia returns to speak to Toshio.

CLAUDIA: Well, I talked to everyone we thought of. A few of them are quite keen, actually.

TOSHIO: Tell me, what did they say?

CLAUDIA: Well, Jennifer can't make it. She's already booked a flight to Queensland. She says she's going to meet her boyfriend up there. I also talked to David Wong. He says he'll come. He says he's really looking forward to getting off campus, too.

TOSHIO: What about his brother, Walter?

CLAUDIA: His brother is going overseas. In fact, he's not even coming back next term. It seems he's transferred to a university in Canada. Er, I then called Maria's house. Her boyfriend, Gyorg, answered. I told him our plans and he asked Maria. They both want to join us.

TOSHIO: Good. They'll be fun to be with. Now, what about Michael Sullivan? Did you talk to him?

CLAUDIA: Yes. But he said he'd rather spend his holiday at home. He's not interested in going anywhere! Can you imagine?

ANNOUNCER: Later, Toshio and Claudia are talking while Toshio fills out a holiday house rental form. Now look at Questions 8 to 11.

(*Pause*)

As the conversation continues, answer Questions 8 to 11.

TOSHIO: The form asks for home addresses. I've put mine, 52 Miller Street, but let me see if I've got yours right. It's 614 Valentine Street, isn't it?

CLAUDIA: You've got the street number right, but not the street name. It's 614 Ballantyne Street. That's B-A-N-T-Y-N-E.

TOSHIO: OK. We're paying by credit card. Is that all right?

CLAUDIA: That's fine.

TOSHIO: Have you got a Visa card or a MasterCard? And I need to know the number, of course.

CLAUDIA: Sure. It's 7743 2129. But it's not a Visa or MasterCard. It's an American Express card.

TOSHIO: So, let me just repeat that. It's 7743 2129. American Express. Right?

CLAUDIA: That's right.

TOSHIO: One more thing we have to write down — that's the deposit we're paying to reserve the holiday house. It says it should be at least 10 per cent of the rental cost.

CLAUDIA: Let's just figure that out now. Er, We're paying $350 a week, right?

TOSHIO: Right. And we're planning to stay there for five weeks. So the deposit's, what, shall we say $225?

CLAUDIA: No, that can't be right. I'd say it's less than that. In fact, about $50 less than that. It should be $175.

TOSHIO: Hmm. I guess you're right. Okay, that's what I'll put down.

ANNOUNCER: That is the end of Section 1. You now have half a minute to check your answers.

Section 2

ANNOUNCER: Listening Section 2. In a moment, you are going to hear an orientation talk given to new overseas students at Maslow University. The talk is being given by Ms Jennifer Davis. Before you listen, look at Questions 12 to 14.

(*Pause*)

As you listen to the first part of the talk, answer Questions 12 to 14.

JENNIFER DAVIS: Hello, my name's Jennifer Davis. I'm the Student Affairs Officer here at Maslow University, and I'd first of all like to welcome you all to this orientation talk. I'll be talking to you about the campus and a little of its history, and then I'll be introducing you to some of the facilities available to all Maslow University students and, in particular, overseas students.

First, let me just point out to you two people who you will definitely need to know. They are Bruce Chandler, who is the coordinator of the Overseas Student Office. Actually, you can see Bruce in that group of people over there. Bruce is the short man with the beard and glasses. Hi, Bruce! Bruce will be speaking to you later.

The other person you'll be meeting is Donna Wilcox. Now, Donna's in charge of the Student Union Activities office. In fact, Donna's just over there, too. She's the one with the white top and dark skirt. Hi there, Donna! She'll be speaking to you today, later, too.

Now, I want to congratulate you all for getting to this talk on time. I say this because I know the campus can be a bit confusing for people when they first get here. In fact, I'd just like to spend a few minutes pointing out some of the landmarks that can be seen from here. Let's see. If you look just behind me, you'll see a large four-storey brick building. That's the Borland Library, named after Harold Borland, who was the first Chancellor of Maslow University. Just ahead of me are two buildings that look like identical twins. In fact, they serve very different purposes. One of them is the University Language Centre. That's the one on my right. The other one — the one on my left — is the Aeronautics Building. Now, to the east of us, you'll see no building at all — just trees and flowers and a huge grassy area. That's the Maslow Gardens, which were part of the original design of the campus. And finally to the west of where I'm standing, we can see the largest building on campus. Seventeen storeys of steel and glass construction. I'll give you one guess what that is. (*laughs*) That's right. It's the University Administration Building.

ANNOUNCER: Now look at Questions 15 to 21.

(*Pause*)

As the talk continues, answer Questions 15 to 21.

JENNIFER DAVIS: Obviously, the buildings we can see from here aren't the only ones on campus. In fact, there are a total of 70 buildings of various sizes and purposes scattered over some 13 hectares of land. Later, I'll be giving out maps to you, and we'll also be giving you a tour after lunch.

Next, let me give you a little history about Maslow University. The University was not originally a university at all. John Herbert Maslow came to this country from Scotland in 1822 at the age of 33. He had trained and worked as a maths teacher before immigrating and when he got here, he found that there were lots of people wanting education, but not nearly enough people to teach them. So he set up a teacher's college on this very site in 1825. The students of the college spent an average of two years here before they went out to find work in primary schools and high schools being set up around the state. Around 3200 students graduated from Maslow Teacher's College in its first ten years of operation. And I should mention that though John Maslow set up the college, it was always strictly a public institution, always the property of the state government.

Now, even though John Maslow died in 1848, the Teacher's College continued to run in much the same way until 1868. Around that time, the state government had plans to establish two new universities. In 1866, Riversdale University was established on a site about 11 kilometres northwest of the city centre. The government wanted the second university to be a bit closer to town, so they chose to convert Maslow Teacher's College into Maslow University. That happened two years after they opened Riversdale University. As you know, Maslow is southeast of the city centre, but it's only 1.5 kilometres away.

You may be interested to know that there's always been an intense rivalry between Maslow University and Riversdale University. They're always trying to outdo each other academically and, also importantly, in sport. Now, with sport, it all depends on what game we're talking about. I don't think anyone in either university would argue that Maslow has the better basketball team and the better soccer team. In fact, Maslow has beaten Riversdale in both sports for about ten years running. But Riversdale University has its strengths, too. Riversdale's football team has always defeated Maslow's, and in women's swimming, too — though not in men's swimming — Riversdale tends to come out on top. When it comes to baseball, well, both universities have a poor record, and the same goes for track and field. Incidentally, the sport teams here at Maslow are always looking for new members, in particular those with a strong background in sport.

Now, let's move on to the facilities in the Student Union ... (*fade out*)

ANNOUNCER: That is the end of Section 2. You now have half a minute to check your answers.

Section 3

ANNOUNCER: Listening Section 3. In a moment, you are going to hear a conversation between Teresa and Bob, two economics students. They are having a cup of coffee between lectures. Before you listen, look at Questions 22 to 33. Note the examples that have been done for you.

(*Pause*)

As you listen to the conversation, answer Questions 22 to 33.

TERESA: Mmm. This is yummy coffee, Bob. How's yours?

BOB: It's excellent. You know, Teresa, I just read an article about coffee last night. It was in that journal that Professor Clark recommended to us.

TERESA: Which one was that? Oh, I think I know. *Food Economics Review*. Isn't that it?

BOB: That's the one. Anyway, in the article there were all kinds of interesting things about coffee that I'd never known before.

TERESA: Yeah? Like what?

BOB: Well, did you know that over 30 million people earn their living from some aspect of coffee farming?

TERESA: That's a lot of people. Coffee obviously has a lot of importance economically.

BOB: Absolutely. In fact, it's the second most valuable commodity in the world after oil.

TERESA: Wow! Well, if it's that big, it's probably produced and controlled by a few large companies, just like with oil.

BOB: Well, this article said otherwise. It said that most coffee's grown by farmers with only 4 or 5 hectares of land. And coffee's usually all they produce.

TERESA: So who produces the most coffee? I mean which country?

BOB: It depends on what type of coffee bean you're talking about.

TERESA: Oh, of course. Each country's coffee has a different flavour. My favourite's Jamaican.

BOB: What you're talking about isn't type; it's just regional variation. What I'm talking about is the coffee bean itself. One common type of coffee bean is called Robusta. It's grown at altitudes of below 600 metres.

TERESA: Is that what we're drinking now?

BOB: Probably not. The coffee we're drinking is premium quality. Robusta is usually used to make instant coffee.

TERESA: Yuck!

BOB: Anyway, the premium coffee — like the stuff we're drinking now — is from a type of bean called Arabica. They grow it higher up, at between 600 and 2000 metres.

TERESA: So those are the two types of coffee, are they?

BOB: Actually, there's one more, called Liberica. It's grown below 1200 metres. But apparently, it's not produced in very large quantities. It's used in blended coffees.

TERESA: Listen, Bob, I'm still waiting for an answer to my question: who grows the most coffee?

BOB: Now that I've explained the types, Teresa, I can tell you. For the Arabica type, it's Brazil followed by Columbia.

TERESA: So Latin America's the biggest producer.

BOB: Only for Arabica coffee. But it's also grown in large quantities in Africa, too. In fact, the number three Arabica producer is Kenya.

TERESA: What about the other type, er, Robusta?

BOB: The biggest producer of Robusta is Uganda. But the second largest is in Asia. That's Indonesia. In fact, Indonesia is the fourth largest producer of coffee, in general, in the world.

TERESA: So, tell me, Bob. Did the article talk about how people like their coffee?

BOB: Yes, it did: in terms of preferred styles of coffee in different countries. The article divided these styles into instant coffee, espresso coffee and brewed coffee. It seems European countries tend to drink more brewed coffee. Countries like Sweden and Norway, for example. It's the same for the Germans. But strangely enough in the UK, instant coffee is king. Perhaps they like the convenience of instant.

TERESA: What about the Italians? I suppose espresso would be what they prefer.

BOB: That's right. And while espresso's popular across the border in France, too, it's still outsold by brewed. In the US, people drink more cups of instant than anything else. But, interestingly enough, in Japan, brewed coffee is the number one.

TERESA: What about the producing countries?

BOB: Well, you're never going to believe this, Teresa, but Brazilians, for example, who grow all those beautiful premium beans, actually prefer instant. It's even more expensive than brewed!

TERESA: Is there any sort of large world body that watches over all the buying and selling of coffee? Like they've got for oil?

BOB: There is. It's called the International Coffee Organisation — the ICO. It was actually set up by the United Nations in 1963 to try to stabilise the world coffee market. There's something like over 100 countries that belong to it, both producing countries and consuming countries.

TERESA: So how does it work?

BOB: It's pretty complex from what I could gather from the article. But basically, the ICO reckons that by controlling the amount of coffee that's available on the world market, they can keep prices from going too low or too high.

TERESA: That sounds reasonable. Does it work?

BOB: Usually, but sometimes it doesn't. Back in 1975, Brazil produced almost no coffee at all because the coffee plants were killed before harvest by freezing weather.

TERESA: Which meant that there was a demand but not much supply.

BOB: Exactly. Especially with Brazil being such a large producer. Anyway, as you'd expect, prices shot through the roof. The ICO couldn't do anything to help.

TERESA: So people paid a premium for coffee, then.

BOB: Well, no, actually. The prices went so high for half a year or so that millions of people no longer bought coffee. They couldn't afford to. So you know what happened next?

TERESA: What? No, let me guess. Er, if nobody's buying coffee, the price had to come down, am I right?

BOB: Exactly right. The whole market collapsed, as a matter of fact, and coffee became cheaper than it had been for the previous 25 years. Unbelievable but true.

TERESA: Shall we order another cup?

ANNOUNCER: That is the end of Section 3. You now have half a minute to check your answers.

Section 4

ANNOUNCER: Listening Section 4. In a moment, you are going to hear a talk given by Katherine Blakely, who is a lecturer in Management Studies. She will be discussing aspects of business meetings. Before you listen, look at Questions 34 to 41. Note the example that has been done for you.

(*Pause*)

As you listen to the talk, answer Questions 34 to 41.

KATHERINE BLAKELY: Hello, everyone. My name's Katherine Blakely. I'm Associate Professor of Management Studies here on campus. Today is the second in our series of talks on aspects of holding business meetings. Last week we talked about the most effective ways of leading meetings, and the advantages and disadvantages of different leadership styles.

Today, in this second talk of the series, I'd like to discuss the role of the facilitator in a meeting. For those of you who aren't aware, businesses and organisations in the past 20 years or so have turned to this idea of a facilitator. A facilitator is a person in the organisation who's chosen to ensure that meetings are carried out efficiently. The facilitator works together with a meeting leader, but their roles are quite different. The meeting leader concerns himself or herself with the *content* of the meeting; by content, I mean, of course, what the meeting's for. The facilitator, on the other hand, is more concerned with the *process* of the meeting. This notion of process includes the rules for the meeting and making sure everyone has a chance to participate.

OK. I next want to outline what are commonly known as the five global responsibilities of a facilitator. This is to give you a better idea of just what a facilitator does and why they're so important to meetings. One global responsibility is labelled 'blueprinting'. Blueprinting a meeting involves creating an agenda and clarifying rules for the meeting. Much of this work is done together with the meeting leader. Blueprinting also means learning about each of the participants and what their goals and interests are with regard to the topic of the meeting. It also involves printing and photocopying documents for the meeting and assembling equipment such as visual aids.

A second global responsibility is what we call 'pro-integration'. Pro-integration happens during the actual meeting. For this, the facilitator must listen carefully to what the participants are saying, then clarify any unfamiliar terms or phrases spoken by the participants. He or she then summarises what was said to ensure everybody at the meeting both fully understands and is fully understood.

Global responsibility number three is what I term 'focusing'. This is basically seeing that everyone keeps to the task at hand, not wandering off onto other topics. It's all too easy for discussion in a meeting to get off track. Here, the facilitator supervises the discussion, making sure all comments are relevant to the task. Focusing also involves knowing in which direction the meeting should be going, and making sure it goes there. We can compare the facilitator's role here to that of a bus driver, steering the group where they need to go.

This brings us to 'prompting', which is our fourth global responsibility. Not everyone at a meeting may feel confident enough to talk, and we must remember that just because they're quiet, it doesn't mean that they've got nothing to contribute. So a facilitator might prompt people, that is, ask people questions or use other activities to get members involved. The task of 'prompting' also means making sure that participants who tend to dominate allow the quieter members a chance to speak. After all, there's nothing more boring than having one or two people dominate a meeting.

When participants get into disputes or arguments with each other, then it's time for the facilitator to take on the role of 'friction manager'. This is the fifth global responsibility of the facilitator, and the last on our list. Friction management means handling conflicts in a positive and constructive manner. During meetings when members may have very different points of view, emotions can run high and people may begin to act negatively toward one another, getting into arguments or what have you. A good facilitator knows that this kind of negative behaviour serves no purpose at business meetings. Its effects are not constructive. So he or she then has to use his or her skills to return the group to a peaceful atmosphere, and maintain that atmosphere. There are various skills involved in friction management which I won't go into here, but basically, the notion of getting the group to focus on what they agree on — rather than what they disagree on — is vital.

ANNOUNCER: That is the end of Section 4. You now have half a minute to check your answers.

(*Pause*)

That is the end of Listening Test 1.

At the end of the real test, you will have ten minutes to transfer your answers to a listening answer sheet.

Section 1

ANNOUNCER: Listening Section 1. In a moment, you will hear a conversation between two university students, William and Mary. It is their first day at the university, and they will both be attending the same lecture this morning. Before you listen, look at Questions 1 to 6.

(*Pause*)

First, William and Mary try to locate the lecture theatre. As you listen to the first part of the conversation, answer Questions 1 to 6.

WILLIAM: Well, Mary. How does it feel on your first day on campus?

MARY: I'm a little nervous, actually. It's such a large campus, and I'm not quite sure how to get around it. How about you?

WILLIAM: I feel the same way. That's why I think we should leave early — to get to our history lecture on time.

MARY: That sounds like a good idea to me! Look, it's 8.15 now. When's the lecture supposed to start, again?

WILLIAM: Er, in 45 minutes. I know it's early, but better safe than sorry, I guess. We've got to go to the Bradley Building, but I'm not sure where that is.

MARY: Since neither of us seems sure how to get there, why don't we ask that man sitting over there. He looks like he may know his way around here.

WILLIAM: All right. I'll ask him.

WILLIAM: Excuse me. Could you tell us how to get to the Bradley Building?

MAN: The Bradley Building? Certainly. Do you see those two buildings over there? The one on the right is the Student Union Building. The other one is the Physics Building. You have to take the path between the two buildings. When you get to the other side of the two buildings, you turn right. From there, the Bradley Building is the second building on your left. Got it?

MARY: I think so. After we get past the Physics and Student Union Buildings, we go right and continue to the second building on the left. Is that right?

MAN: That's right.

ANNOUNCER: William and Mary later arrive in the lobby of the Bradley Building.

MARY: Well, we've got here in good time. Do you know which theatre the lecture's in?

WILLIAM: It's supposed to be in Lecture Theatre H, I think. Wherever that is! There are at least ten floors in this building! Shall we ask somebody for directions again?

MARY: I don't think we'll need to. There's a directory next to the stairs over there. Let's take a look. Let's see. It says here that Lecture Theatres 'A' to 'D' are on the sixth floor, Theatres 'E' and 'F' are on the eighth floor, and the rest of the theatres are on the tenth floor.

WILLIAM: Shall we take the stairs?

MARY: Are you serious? I'm not going to walk up all that way! Let's take that escalator over there.

WILLIAM: Look. You can see it's not moving. If you don't want to walk up, I guess we'll have to find a lift.

MARY: Actually, I noticed a sign when we came into the building that said the lifts weren't working on the ground and first floors. I suppose we'd better take the stairs to the second floor and take the lift from there.

WILLIAM: Okay, let's go.

ANNOUNCER: Mary and William arrive at Lecture Theatre H.

MARY: Well, we've finally made it. And we started out exactly 40 minutes ago! I hope it doesn't take us so long next time.

WILLIAM: Yes, if we can just memorise the way we got here.

MARY: Hey, William. That's strange; there's no one here! Are you sure this is the right place?

WILLIAM: Yes, I'm sure. Hey, wait a moment! There's a sign posted on the blackboard. Can you see what it says?

MARY: Yeah, it says the professor's sick. And that there'll be no lecture today. I guess that means we've come all the way to this lecture theatre for nothing!

ANNOUNCER: Later, Mary and William discuss Mary's timetable for the rest of the week. Now look at Questions 7 to 11. Note the examples that have been done for you.

(*Pause*)

As the conversation continues, answer Questions 7 to 11.

WILLIAM: You've got a rather busy week ahead of you, haven't you?

MARY: Yeah, I've got two lectures on Tuesday. One's a chemistry lecture at 10 a.m. and the other's microbiology at 2 o'clock. The microbiology lecture goes for one hour, and then it's followed immediately by a lab.

WILLIAM: What lab is that?

MARY: Er, plant pathology.

WILLIAM: That sounds like quite a full day.

MARY: Well, actually, Wednesday's my busiest. I've got two tutorials, a lecture and a chemistry lab. The lab's first thing in the morning at 9 o'clock. That goes until 11 o'clock. Then, my first tutorial, that's plant pathology, is at 12. I get a couple of hours break for lunch and relaxation. Then at 3 o'clock I've got another tutorial, er, my microbiology tutorial. That goes for two hours. Finally, at 5 o'clock, I've got my genetics lecture.

WILLIAM: Whew, I see what you mean about Wednesday being your busiest day. What about the rest of the week?

MARY: Well, I've got nothing on on Thursday, thankfully. And Friday's a short day; I've just got a lecture — plant pathology. And the best thing is that it begins at 10 o'clock in the morning. So from 11 o'clock, I'm free to enjoy the weekend!

ANNOUNCER: That is the end of Section 1. You now have half a minute to check your answers.

Section 2

ANNOUNCER: Listening Section 2. In a moment, you are going to hear a talk given by Ms Margaret Sayles, a travel writer. She will be talking about travel to the Pacific island country of Astoria. Before you listen, look at Questions 12 to 15. An example has been provided for you.

(Pause)

As you listen to the first part of the talk, answer Questions 12 to 15.

MARGARET SAYLES: Good morning, everyone. My name's Margaret Sayles. I'm a journalist who specialises in travel. Some of you may read the travel section of the newspaper, so you know the kinds of articles I write.

Anyway, I'm not here to tell you about my job. I've been invited here by the Astoria Tourism Bureau to tell you about travel to Astoria. Now as I'm sure most of you know, Astoria is a rather large island located eleven hundred kilometres from New Zealand. That's eleven hundred kilometres in a northeast direction, I should say. As you can see on this map here, it's about 25 per cent larger than New Zealand, and it has quite a different shape. While New Zealand's long and thin, Astoria has the shape of a rectangle — some people would say almost square.

Now, I guess none of you here has been to Astoria yet, so let me give you a bit of a description. Most of the people there live in the northern half of the island. This part of the island is warmer than the southern half, but it wouldn't be fair to say that the southern half is cold. In fact, the whole island is close enough to the Equator so that no matter how far south you go, you wouldn't even need a jumper to stay warm.

ANNOUNCER: Now look at Questions 16 to 23. Note the examples that have been done for you.

(Pause)

As the talk continues, answer Questions 16 to 23.

MARGARET SAYLES: There are four provinces in Astoria. Each has its own unique features and, in fact, one of them speaks a different language. The northwest quarter of the country is the province of Hornchurch. The capital of the country, which is called New Birmingham, is located in Hornchurch and that's where the first English settlers came in the year 1756. New Birmingham is Astoria's largest city and the centre of its industry. And it's the culture of this part of the island that attracts so many tourists to Hornchurch. The culture's a strange mix of old English and Polynesian. New Birmingham is where you'll most likely enter the country if you're going by air because it has the busiest airport. Hornchurch's population is 2.5 million.

The second largest province in terms of population is New Devon. It's got half a million people fewer than Hornchurch. New Devon takes up the northeast quarter of the country. Now if you're the type of person who likes the beach, this is the best part of the island. The beaches are absolutely beautiful here and they go on for miles. There are beach resorts all along the coast on this part of the island, and no matter how much money you want to spend on your holiday, there are beach resorts that will suit your budget in New Devon.

South of New Devon is the province of Anglezark. This is the most mountainous part of Astoria, and its least populated. Only a quarter of a million people live here.

The mountains in Anglezark are well known for their hot springs and many Astorians, as well as tourists, go there to rest and relax in the mineral baths. The hot springs are probably the best reason to visit the province, especially if you want to get away from the more crowded beaches of the northeastern part of the island. But take along a good pair of hiking boots if you want to take advantage of the wonderful bushwalking in the Anglezark mountains.

The fourth province of Astoria is in the southwest quarter of the island. It's called New Albion. Now, that may sound deceptively English, but actually that's not the language you're likely to hear in New Albion. Although the English were the first Europeans to come to Astoria, explorers from Spain came only a few months later, and they settled in this part of the island. Today, Spanish is still the main language in New Albion, while people in the other three provinces communicate in English.

Overseas visitors like to come to New Albion to indulge in one of Astoria's more famous agricultural products — wine. I'm sure you know that Astoria's wines are considered to be some of the best in the world. Well, all of the wine produced in Astoria is made in New Albion because the weather here is perfect for it — warm days and cool nights but not too humid. By the way, New Albion has the only other international airport in Astoria so it's possible to arrive there first if you're going by air.

OK. I've briefly told you about the place. Now, let me show you some slides and then I'll tell you about prices and travel arrangements and . . . (*fade out*)

ANNOUNCER: That is the end of Section 2. You now have half a minute to check your answers.

Section 3

ANNOUNCER: Listening Section 3. In a moment, you are going to hear an interview between Ms Marilyn Stokes, a radio interviewer, and Mr Roger Harridan, a scientist working in the field of sensory perception. Before you listen, look at Questions 24 to 33. Note the example done for you.

(*Pause*)

As you listen to the conversation, answer Questions 24 to 33.

MARILYN STOKES (MS): Our next guest is Mr Roger Harridan. Roger is a scientist at the National Institute for Sense and Sensory Perception. He's come here to chat with us about our sense of smell — you know, how we use our nose. How are you today, Roger?

ROGER HARRIDAN (RH): Very well, thank you, Marilyn.

MS: You know, Roger, I love the smell of flowers and good food cooking, but I must admit, I've never really given much thought to my sense of smell.

RH: Well, Marilyn, you're not alone in that. Most people would say their eyesight was their most important sense, but I suspect very few people would consider their nose or the idea of smell in that way.

MS: Unless, of course, you make perfume for a living. (*laughs*)

RH: Yes, indeed. I'm sure most of your listeners would have heard of Immanuel Kant.

MS: Immanuel Kant? The German philosopher, you mean?

RH: That's right. Now Kant, who lived 200 years ago, was the first person we know of to rank the five senses in order of importance. Kant put seeing, or eyesight, in the first position. He regarded it as absolutely the most important sense. Now, what do you think he chose for number two?

MS: Oh, I really don't know. But if it were me, I'd choose hearing, I suppose.

RH: Well, that's exactly what Kant chose, as well. For the third most important sense, he chose touch. And touch was followed by taste.

MS: Which leaves smell on the very bottom.

RH: I'm afraid so. But this was simply the opinion of one man, of course. Actually, Kant was interested in the ideas of subjectivity and objectivity. He put smell last because he felt that it was subjective. He thought the senses of seeing and hearing and touch were objective, while taste and smell, he said, were subjective senses. He even went so far as to say that we humans don't need our sense of smell, that we can easily live without it. He obviously didn't have much use for these subjective senses.

MS: Well, I can't say I agree with him on that last point. Roger, how well can people smell?

RH: Well, most people have quite normal, quite acceptable abilities to smell. I mean, if there was a gas leak in this room, for example, the average person would notice fairly quickly. But some people are known as 'odour-blind'. Such people can't smell certain odours, certain smells. Just like people who are colour-blind may not be able to see a particular colour. An odour-blind person may be able to enjoy the smell of one kind of flower just as you or I would, but another kind of flower that you or I think smells wonderful, well, they wouldn't be able to smell a thing.

MS: How extraordinary!

RH: It is, isn't it? Another thing about our sense of smell: as we get older, many of us are less and less able to use our nose.

MS: How old do you mean?

RH: Well, about half of people over the age of 65 have some sort of trouble smelling things. And as you age even more, the sense weakens more. So, for people over 80, we can expect some three-quarters to have problems with their ability to smell. And what's more, if you're a man, you can expect to have a weaker sense of smell than if you're a woman.

MS: Roger, we were talking about perfume earlier. Now, there's a huge industry based on people's sense of smell.

RH: Yes, well, perfume is certainly big business. I read recently that in the United States alone, they sell $4.8 billion worth of perfume every year. And in Japan, the yearly sales are something like $5.5 billion— the world's biggest marketplace for the stuff.

MS: I've always wondered what makes some people use certain perfumes.

RH: I would say the number one reason is that they like the smell. But that's followed closely by reason number two, Marilyn. They think it's fashionable. Perfumes that people see as fashionable sell well. Just ask any of the big fashion companies. But the interesting thing about perfume is that one brand of perfume doesn't smell the same on every person who uses it.

MS: Yes, I've noticed that before. Why is that?

RH: Scientists don't know why for certain. Researchers in France think it has something to do with the liver. That is, the condition of your liver determines how the perfume will smell on you. But other scientists aren't too sure of that theory.

MS: Isn't it also true that each person smells the same perfume differently?

RH: It's hard to say because, for example, you and I might smell a perfume and, though we have the same sensation of the odour of the perfume, I may think it's a lovely smell and you may think it smells like last week's dinner!

MS: (*laughs*) I see what you mean. It's partly a matter of like and dislike, then, isn't it, Roger?

RH: That's right. In fact, there are people who dislike perfumes in general — any perfume. They feel it's an intrusion — you know, like cigarette smoke.

MS: Wait; let me guess. You're going to tell me next that we're going to have anti-perfume campaigns, sort of like the campaigns against cigarette smoking indoors that've been so successful in so many places.

RH: That's what I predict will happen, Marilyn. In fact, it's already begun in the United States, where, I've heard . . . (*fade out*)

ANNOUNCER: That is the end of Section 3. You now have half a minute to check your answers.

Section 4

ANNOUNCER: Listening Section 4. You are attending a talk for overseas students on greeting customs in Australia. The speaker is Mr Geoff Barker, an anthropologist. Before you listen, look at Questions 34 to 42. An example has been done for you.

(*Pause*)

As you listen to the talk, answer Questions 34 to 42.

GEOFF BARKER: Think about how you greet someone for the first time in your own country, in your own culture. When you're introduced to a stranger, do you shake hands with him or her? Perhaps it isn't the custom to touch each other. Instead, you may simply bow to each other, or make no gesture at all.

You know what to do in your own country, but what about when you go overseas for study or business? I've met many students who told me they were sometimes confused about these things in the first weeks after arriving here. And that's why I've been asked to give this talk to you today.

Let's look at the act of shaking hands — and what I'm about to say applies mainly to men. When you're introduced to someone in a formal situation here in Australia, you always shake hands with them. And in an informal situation, it's quite common, too. Shaking hands is the most accepted way of touching someone you don't know (and the idea of touching them is in itself important). If you *don't* shake someone's hand when they are clearly expecting it, the message you are sending is that you're not interested in them. So, fellows, I advise you to shake hands here, even if you don't normally do so in your own country.

If you think that simply shaking hands is enough, though, then you'd better listen to what I have to say next. *How* you shake hands is almost as important as the act itself. *How* you shake hands tells the other person a lot about you. It's true, and especially so of men!

Here's what I mean. A limp or weak handshake by a man has the same meaning as no handshake at all. The message is: 'I'm not very interested in you.' Think about this, because I know that some of you may come from cultures that accept limp handshakes as normal. Here, even if you don't intend to, you may send the wrong message.

Is the best way, then, to use all your muscles and crush — and possibly hurt — the other person's hand? Man-to-man handshakes in Australia are sometimes like this. The message behind this kind of handshake is aggressiveness and a desire to compete. Unless you specifically want to communicate these feelings to the other person, you don't have to shake hands with all your strength. One more type of male handshake that can send the wrong message is the half handshake. Here, only the front half of the fingers is offered to the other person's hand. The message is that you have little confidence, that you're shy. 'I'm not a strong or courageous person.' That's what a half handshake says.

Let's look now at how it is for women. Until recently, women in Australia felt no great need to shake hands during introductions. That's changed as more and more women are working in business, government and academia. The way that women used to shake hands with men was to give only half the hand — that is, the fingers only. This gave little impression or message, at least to men. Nowadays, women are having to learn again how to shake hands. Now, women are beginning to offer all of the hand — the fingers and palm. The other person's hand is held and shaken firmly but not too hard. This communicates to the other person more of a feeling of competence or strength than the old-fashioned way of doing it.

How long *should* you shake hands? That's right; the *length of time* you shake hands also says something about you. If a man lets go of the other person's hand too quickly, what kind of message do you think that sends? Releasing your hand quite soon indicates that you don't want to get too involved or you're not very interested in the other person. That goes for both women and men. However, it's both more acceptable and more common for two men to shake hands for a longer time, even as long as six or seven seconds. The message in this case is 'I like you' and generally indicates that the two men think they'll get on well.

Finally, what do you do with your eyes when you are shaking a stranger's hand? In this society at least, you should look at the other person straight in the eyes. If you look somewhere else, like looking down or to the side, this sends a negative message to the other person. The other person may think you are being arrogant, that your action says 'I am better than you'. Another unpleasant message that comes across when there is no eye contact is: 'You don't exist' or 'I don't recognise your existence.'

So you see, there really is quite a lot to consider when shaking hands in this culture. As silly as it may sound, practising handshaking, say with a friend, may be a good way to become confident so that the next time you need to introduce yourself in a formal setting here in Australia, you'll feel comfortable knowing you did it the right way.

ANNOUNCER: That is the end of Section 4. You now have half a minute to check your answers.

(*Pause*)

That is the end of Listening Test 2.

At the end of the real test, you will have ten minutes to transfer your answers to a listening answer sheet.

Paper Three

Section 1

ANNOUNCER: Listening Section 1. In a moment, you are going to hear a conversation between two university students, Vincent and Sareena. They are meeting on their university campus. Before you listen, look at Questions 1 to 5.

(*Pause*)

As you listen to the first part of the conversation, answer Questions 1 to 5.

SAREENA: Hi, Vincent. How are you?

VINCENT: Hello there, Sareena. I'm well, thank you. I haven't seen you for ages! How've you been?

SAREENA: Good, thanks. I see you've just walked out of the Life Sciences Building. You're not taking classes in biology or something, are you? I thought you were studying sociology.

VINCENT: I am studying sociology, Sareena. I was just visiting a friend of mine who's doing research in biochemistry. Actually, I'm on my way to lunch and then I've got a lecture.

SAREENA: Oh, well, look. I was just going to have a bite to eat as well. Shall we have something together?

VINCENT: That would be great.

SAREENA: The problem with this campus is that the town's so far away, which is where I prefer to eat. It seems like all the students are forced to eat here on campus.

VINCENT: Yeah, but there are quite a few places to choose from here. What if we go to the Student Union cafeteria? I go there sometimes. At least it's cheap.

SAREENA: Yes, the Union cafeteria's cheap, Vincent, but you get what you pay for! That's one place I try to avoid as much as possible. I only go there when I'm low on money or when they have live music. Besides, it's too crowded around lunchtime, and . . .

VINCENT: All right, all right . . . I know! How about the Aztec Grill? Do you know that one? It's on the third floor of the Arts Centre.

SAREENA: The Aztec Grill, huh? I think I've seen it, but I've never been there. Doesn't it specialise in Mexican food or something?

VINCENT: Yes, it's pretty spicy. Do you like spicy food?

SAREENA: Actually, I love spicy things, but I shouldn't be eating them at the moment. I just got over a stomach flu, so I'd prefer something mild.

VINCENT: I haven't got a problem with that. I guess I better let you pick a place, then. Where would you like to go?

SAREENA: How about the Luxor Cafe?

VINCENT: The Luxor Cafe? You know, I've been on campus for over two years and I don't think I've ever heard of it. Where is it?

SAREENA: It's in the garden behind the Horticulture Annex.

VINCENT: The Horticulture Annex. That's in the northwest part of campus, isn't it?

SAREENA: No, it's south of the Observatory.

VINCENT: So, it's near the football field, then? Behind Carpark 'C'?

SAREENA: Not quite that far south. It's west of the Law Library.

VINCENT: Oh, right. I think I know where that is. It's not very far at all. Let's go!

ANNOUNCER: Later, Vincent and Sareena sit in the Luxor Cafe, deciding what to eat. Now look at Questions 6 to 11. One example has been done for you.

(*Pause*)

As the conversation continues, answer Questions 6 to 11.

VINCENT: Well, the menu's quite extensive, isn't it? I feel like I could spend hours deciding what to order.

SAREENA: Yes, I know what you mean ... I think I'll have a salad to start with.

VINCENT: But there are so many salads to choose from!

SAREENA: Yeah, but I know what I like. I'll order the Greek salad.

VINCENT: If you know this place so well, I'd better follow your example. I'll have a Greek salad, too.

SAREENA: Hey, wait a sec. If you order a different kind, we can share and have a greater variety.

VINCENT: All right. That sounds good to me. Er, how about if I have a seafood salad, then?

SAREENA: Good choice. They use fresh ingredients here, so you won't be disappointed. I'm quite hungry, so I'll have a sandwich, too. A chicken sandwich.

VINCENT: I think I'll have some soup. Is the onion soup any good?

SAREENA: I don't know. I've never ordered it. It's not my favourite soup, to be honest. Why don't you try the tomato soup? I've had it here lots of times.

VINCENT: No, I think I'll stick with the onion. And I think I'll have a sandwich as well. You reckon the chicken's good, eh?

SAREENA: If you like chicken sandwiches, yes. The roast beef's quite tasty, too.

VINCENT: No, I'll go with the chicken.

SAREENA: That's a lot of food you're ordering, Vincent. Are you sure you can get through all that?

VINCENT: (*laughs*) Not a problem. I could eat a horse. Shall we order now? Oh, we still have to choose something to drink.

SAREENA: I'll have lemon tea. They say lemon tea's good for the stomach, which is what I need.

VINCENT: I'll have mineral water, myself.

ANNOUNCER: After eating, Vincent and Sareena leave the cafe.

SAREENA: Well, it was nice having lunch with you, Vincent.

VINCENT: Yes, have you got time to meet for lunch again next week, perhaps?

SAREENA: I don't see why not. Tuesdays and Fridays are bad for me though. I've got tutorials and labs around lunch time on those days. But I'm on campus every day, so . . .

VINCENT: I've got the same problem on Tuesdays, Thursdays and Fridays. I guess that leaves us with Monday or Wednesday.

SAREENA: Let's make it Monday. Why don't we meet here at the Luxor Cafe? Say, around 1.15?

VINCENT: You wouldn't want to make it a bit earlier, would you? Like 12.30 or 12.45? It would be better for me.

SAREENA: Well, I finish a lecture at 12.15, and I usually stick around to talk to the lecturer. But I guess quarter to one would be all right.

VINCENT: Good. Then it's settled. I'll see you then.

ANNOUNCER: That is the end of Section 1. You now have half a minute to check your answers.

Section 2

ANNOUNCER: Listening Section 2. In a moment, you are going to hear a talk given by Mr Alf Meerschaum, who works as a real estate agent in the city of Chapmanville. He is speaking to a group of newcomers about the city and rental accommodation to be found there. Before you listen, look at Questions 12 to 22. Note the examples that have been done for you.

(*Pause*)

As you listen to the talk, answer Questions 12 to 22.

ALF MEERSCHAUM: Hi, I'm Alf Meerschaum. I'm the rental manager for the Central Chapmanville Real Estate Agency. I'm a real estate agent much like any other in that I help people buy and sell houses, but about half my time is spent working to assist people in renting houses and flats. I've been in this business for a dozen years now, and I know this city very well in terms of which areas are the better places to live and how much it costs to rent in these areas.

Now, I normally divide Chapmanville into three areas in terms of rental prices. Generally speaking, the area in the north of the city is the low end of the spectrum, the cheapest housing. So if you're looking to spend as little as possible on rent, I suggest you look there. The most expensive area would be the eastern part of Chapmanville. Most people think it's the prettiest part of the metropolitan area because of all the hills and parks. And because so many people desire to live there, housing prices tend to be quite high. The middle market in terms of prices for accommodation is found in the city's western and southern areas.

Now, let me give you some examples of how much it will cost you to rent in these areas. Let's imagine you're a single person looking for a one-bedroom flat. In eastern Chapmanville, you would be paying no less than $650 a month for such a flat. You won't find anything for less than that. But a lot of people pay as much as $1100 per month or more. The higher-priced flats are usually the ones in the hills, which run through the east. They've got the best views of the city.

A similarly sized flat in the west of the city — and in the south, too, for that matter — would cost you at most about $650 a month, but there are many flats going for less, and if you look around a bit, you can find one for as little as $350. That's quite a reasonable rental price for most people. If you still find that too expensive, I suggest you head to Chapmanville's north, where the cheapest flats are to be found. One-bedroom flats there start from about $170 a month up to about $400.

Now, for those of you who want something bigger, you'll have to be prepared to pay about double those prices for a small two- or three-bedroom house. That goes for any of the areas I mentioned.

Okay, so much for prices. What are the advantages and disadvantages of these areas? Well, I told you that the eastern part of Chapmanville is the prettiest. There are lots of parks and lots of trees all around. And you've got the beautiful hills right there.

In the south, you've also got the river, but you won't find too many parks there, because of all the factories alongside the river. In fact, there's quite a bit of industry in the south, which makes it a less desirable place to live. Still, the south is convenient because of public transport. The south has very good train services to the city centre as well as buses, and that's why a lot of people choose to live there.

I said earlier that the western and southern parts of Chapmanville are about the same in terms of the price you pay for accommodation. They also have the same sort of public transport services. But, the two areas are quite different in other ways. The west is next to the bay, so it's quite attractive in that sense. But there are a couple of problems with the west. One is that the bay is polluted. So polluted, in fact, that you wouldn't want to swim there. I used to take my family there about ten years ago, but now I wouldn't go near it. The other disadvantage of the west is that that's where the airport is. The Chapmanville International Airport. The noise can be quite annoying.

Lastly, the north. In northern Chapmanville, as I said before, housing is cheap. Quite cheap, in fact. But you pay in other ways. For example, the area is very low and is made up entirely of wetlands. It's beautiful in a way, but it attracts an incredible amount of insects for most of the year. The mosquitoes there are really bad. This makes things quite unpleasant, and so few people have any real wish to live there. But, if money's a problem, that's the place to go. Just bring your insect repellent!

Oh, I should mention that the only public transport in the north is buses; there aren't any trains. So, it's not all that convenient, as you can imagine. Actually, eastern Chapmanville is in the same situation in terms of public transport, even though it's a richer part of the city. Don't ask me why that is, though.

Let me just finish by again welcoming you all to Chapmanville and wishing you good luck in finding accommodation and settling down in whichever part of the city suits you best.

ANNOUNCER: That is the end of Section 2. You now have half a minute to check your answers.

Section 3

ANNOUNCER: Listening Section 3. In a moment, you are going to hear a conversation between three students, Wanda, Jack and Annette. They are reviewing their lecture notes after hearing a lecture on the subject of bottle recycling. Before you listen, look at Questions 23 to 32. Note the example that has been done for you.

(Pause)

As you listen to the conversation, answer Questions 23 to 32.

JACK: Hello, Wanda. Hello, Annette. I had trouble getting out of bed this morning so I came to class a bit late. I got to the lecture theatre about 30 minutes after Professor Johnson began her lecture. Do you mind telling me what I missed?

WANDA: Not at all, Jack. Actually, you didn't miss more than 15 minutes because Professor Johnson arrived a bit late herself.

ANNETTE: Which is pretty typical for her, isn't it?

(*all laugh*)

WANDA: It sure is. Let's see. How do your notes begin, Jack?

JACK: Er. Well, when I came in she was talking about recycling of cans, and the differences between can and bottle recycling.

WANDA: Right, okay. Well, before that, she explained a little about glass bottle recycling. She said that glass recycling is still far more efficient than recycling other materials. That's because there's no loss of quality no matter how many times the glass is recycled.

JACK: Hmm. That's interesting.

WANDA: She also talked about the tiny little pieces of glass you get when you break up bottles in the recycling process. What's that called again, Annette?

ANNETTE: It's called 'cullet'. It's spelled 'C-U-double-L-E-T'.

WANDA: Yes, that's right. The professor said that there are bottle factories in some parts of the world, like Japan and the US, that make their bottles entirely from cullet.

JACK: So, they don't use new glass.

ANNETTE: That's right.

JACK: What about bottle factories elsewhere?

ANNETTE: Er. Let me just check my notes. (*paper rustling*) Er, the bottles made in most places contain about three-quarters new glass and the rest is recycled.

JACK: I guess recycling is better for the environment than just throwing things away and using new materials all the time, but wouldn't it be even better to reuse the same bottles without breaking them up into cullet?

WANDA: Yeah, Professor Johnson talked about that, too. She said if you reuse bottles you save on energy and resource costs. She said that in parts of Britain, beer bottles are still reused rather than recycled. But she said that reusable bottles have to be built stronger than the kinds of bottles that are recycled after they're used only once.

JACK: But then they last forever, don't they?

WANDA: Actually, no. Reusable bottles can be cleaned and refilled a maximum of 30 times, and then they become too weak to use again. They're crushed and recycled.

JACK: But it still sounds better than just recycling. My parents tell me that when they were children, a lot more things came in reusable bottles and jars. It really seems like we've moved away from reusing, doesn't it? Did Professor Johnson talk about why that's so?

WANDA: Well, she discussed why it's so difficult to maintain a system of returning and reusing bottles.

JACK: What reasons did she mention?

WANDA: Well, a few things. One factor is that there's an increasing variety of bottle types on the market. You know, when you walk into a supermarket, you see virtually hundreds of different types of drinks, and each one has its own bottle shape and colour. In other words, there is virtually no standardisation. And standardisation is necessary to keep a bottle reusing system going. It gets too complicated and expensive to have a separate scheme for each bottle type.

JACK: That makes sense. So we're paying for the variety of bottles by having to recycle them rather than reuse them.

WANDA: I guess that's right. But that's not the only problem. Apparently, shopkeepers are another obstacle. They don't want to have to collect all the returned bottles. Shopkeepers claim they can't afford the time it takes and that it's not their responsibility anyway.

JACK: I suppose I can see their point in a way. But, in terms of the environment, it's not a very caring attitude, is it?

WANDA: No. But things may be changing. Professor Johnson said that governments are beginning to realise the need to cut down on wastes. So some places are making laws that require everyone to return their bottles for reuse. It's happening in Denmark and in parts of Canada. In those countries, a person who buys something in a bottle, like a soft drink, is responsible for returning the bottle once they've finished with it. If they don't, they're breaking the law. Also, bottle makers aren't allowed to make bottles that cannot be reused.

JACK: That's encouraging. Anything else?

WANDA: Well, she then talked about plastic bottles. She said that it's still better environmentally to buy things packaged in glass bottles, because recycling them is more efficient. But there are relatively recent programs for recycling plastics. And recycling plastics has its advantages.

JACK: Such as?

WANDA: She said that recycling of plastic uses one-tenth the energy of creating new plastic.

JACK: Only a tenth of the energy, did you say? Wow, so recycling plastics has its benefits, too.

ANNETTE: Finally, she said that we should also look at other factors about bottle use, too, like transportation. Obviously, there's an environmental cost in transporting bottles to and from factories and shops. She said plastics are better than glass in this respect because they're lighter. For glass, one tonne is about 2000 average bottles. For plastic, it's ten times that. That's 20 000 bottles per tonne.

JACK: That's quite a difference, isn't it? Maybe plastic is the way to go, after all.

ANNOUNCER: That is the end of Section 3. You now have half a minute to check your answers.

Section 4

ANNOUNCER: Listening Section 4. In a moment, you are going to hear a talk about stress and its effects. The talk is being given by a psychologist, Dr Fiona Williams. Before you listen, look at Questions 33 to 36.

(*Pause*)

As you listen to the first part of the talk, answer Questions 33 to 36.

DR FIONA WILLIAMS: We're here today to talk a little about stress — that is, mental or emotional stress. It's something we can't entirely avoid, and yet we need to be aware of its effects on us when it builds up to dangerous levels.

Stress is quite usual among university students. Of course, you know the more obvious sources of stress: a deadline for an essay or a project, for example, can certainly be a source. Especially as the day gets near. Also, the feeling you might have when you have to speak to many people at once. That can bring on stress as well. But there are other, less obvious reasons, too. Stress can come when you're listening to a lecture and trying to keep up with the lecturer's words as you take notes. (*laughs*) In fact, you might be feeling stress as you're listening to me right now! Another stressful situation for the university student is waiting for results. After you hand in your paper, for example, you have to wait a while before you know how you've done and that period of time can be very difficult. One more source of stress is burnout — the feeling you get from working too long and too hard at your assignments. Burnout happens on the job and at school, especially. It's also important to remember that not all the stress you may be feeling has to do with your studies. In fact, there are plenty more sources of stress in our day-to-day lives. Things to do with family or work, for example.

ANNOUNCER: Now look at Questions 37 to 39. One example has been done for you.

(*Pause*)

As the talk continues, answer Questions 37 to 39.

DR FIONA WILLIAMS: But perhaps the most stressful things of all are major life events. When somebody you know dies. That's a big one. Or, more happily, when you're having a baby. That causes a lot of stress, too.

Now, in 1969, a psychologist by the name of Thomas Holmes came up with what he called a 'life event stress index'. Now how this stress index works is like this. For every important event in your life, there is a number — a score if you like. The higher the score, the more stressful the event. The highest number is 100, which represents the most stressful experience you can have. Do you understand so far? Now, Holmes divided these events into three categories, depending on their score. Events scoring under 35 points he called 'moderately stressful'. Events between 35 and 65 he labelled 'highly stressful'. And everything scoring above that was called 'extremely stressful'.

Okay, let me read you a few of these so you understand what I'm talking about. Getting married gets a score of 51. That's considered quite stressful, especially when you consider the change this brings to your life. It's not as stressful, though, as when you get a divorce; that's 73. How about when you get pregnant? That's worth 40 points according to the index. When you finish school you score 26 points. That's exactly the same score — the same stress level — as when your husband or wife leaves his or her job.

ANNOUNCER: Now look at Questions 40 to 43.

(*Pause*)

As the talk continues, answer Questions 40 to 43.

DR FIONA WILLIAMS: Let me read you a few more examples from the stress index. If you move to a new house or flat, the score is 20. You get 45 points if you retire. That's 2 points less than if you get fired from your job. On the other hand, if you find yourself arguing with your mother-in-law, the stress rating is 29 points. How about going on a holiday? When you think about it, a vacation can create stress, too. It gets 13 points.

Now, I'll stop with the scores for a moment. Next, I want to look at what these numbers actually mean. You're supposed to add up the numbers for events that took place within the last 12 months only. The total is supposed to tell us something about how likely we are to get sick, to become ill from the level of stress.

How do we know when we're under a lot of stress? There are many signs, but I'll just mention a few. One is communicating less with friends and family or at work or school. You may not feel like talking to people so much. When the phone rings, you hope it isn't for you. You just don't want to have to deal with other people and their problems. But humans are naturally social animals, and when there is a constant desire to be left alone, there's something wrong, and it's usually a sign of stress.

A second indication is feeling less energy when you wouldn't normally feel tired. You may be eating well or not even studying or working very hard, but you still feel you have very little energy. Like you want to sleep all the time. That's probably stress.

When we have trouble sleeping, this, too, usually means the problem is stress. It might take you a long time to fall asleep, or you may wake up in the middle of the night and not be able to fall asleep again. A person like this is more likely to fall asleep while watching television than in bed!

ANNOUNCER: That is the end of Section 4. You now have half a minute to check your answers.

(*Pause*)

That is the end of Listening Test 3.

At the end of the real test, you will have ten minutes to transfer your answers to the listening answer sheet.